Agriculture, Food & Natural Resources

Daniel Lewis

MASON CREST

Mason Crest
450 Parkway Drive, Suite D
Broomall, PA 19008
www.masoncrest.com

Printed in the United States of America
First printing
9 8 7 6 5 4 3 2 1

Series ISBN: 978-1-4222-4132-5
Hardcover ISBN: 978-1-4222-4136-3

Library of Congress Cataloging-in-Publication Data is available on file.

Developed and Produced by Print Matters Productions, Inc.
(www.printmattersinc.com)
Cover and Interior Design by Lori S Malkin Design, LLC

CAREERS IN DEMAND FOR HIGH SCHOOL GRADUATES

Agriculture, Food & Natural Resources

Armed Forces

Computers, Communications & the Arts

Construction & Trades

Fitness, Personal Care Services & Education

Health Care & Science

Hospitality & Human Services

Public Safety & Law

Sales, Marketing & Finance

Transportation & Manufacturing

KEY ICONS TO LOOK FOR:

 Words to understand: These words with their easy-to-understand definitions will increase the reader's understanding of the text while building vocabulary skills.

 Sidebars: This boxed material within the main text allows readers to build knowledge, gain insights, explore possibilities, and broaden their perspectives by weaving together additional information to provide realistic and holistic perspectives.

 Educational Videos: Readers can view videos by scanning our QR codes, providing them with additional educational content to supplement the text. Examples include news coverage, moments in history, speeches, iconic sports moments and much more!

 Text-dependent Questions: These questions send the reader back to the text for more careful attention to the evidence presented there.

 Research projects: Readers are pointed toward areas of further inquiry connected to each chapter. Suggestions are provided for projects that encourage deeper research and analysis.

INTRODUCTION...6

Chapter 1: Farmworker 9

Chapter 2: Livestock Farmworker 21

Chapter 3: Pest Control Technician/Animal Control Officer................. 33

Chapter 4: Butcher/Various Meat-Processing Occupations 47

Chapter 5: Groundskeeper (Landscaper, Tree Trimmer)..................... 59

Chapter 6: Forestry/Conservation/Logging-Crew Member................. 73

Chapter 7: Nursery/Greenhouse Assistant...................................... 85

Chapter 8: Forest Firefighter/Range Aide 97

INDEX.. 110

PHOTO CREDITS.. 112

For millions of Americans, life after high school means stepping into the real world. Each year more than 1 million of the nation's 3.1 million high school graduates go directly into the workforce. Clearly, college isn't for everyone. Many people learn best by using their hands rather than by sitting in a classroom. Others find that the escalating cost of college puts it beyond reach, at least for the time being. During the 2016–2017 school year, for instance, tuition and fees at a "moderate" four-year, in-state public college averaged $24,610, not including housing costs, according to The College Board.

The good news is that there's a wide range of exciting, satisfying careers available without a four-year bachelor's degree or even a two-year associate's degree. Careers in Demand for High School Graduates highlights specific, in-demand careers in which individuals who have only a high school diploma or the General Educational Development (GED) credential can find work, with or without further training (outside of college).

These jobs span the range from apprentice electronics technician to chef, teacher's assistant, Web page designer, sales associate, and lab technician. The additional training that some of these positions require may be completed either on the job, through a certificate program, or during an apprenticeship that combines entry-level work and class time. Happily, there's plenty of growth in the number of jobs that don't require a college diploma, though that growth is fastest for positions that call for additional technical training or a certificate of proficiency.

So, what career should a high school graduate consider? The range is so broad that Careers in Demand for High School Graduates includes 10 volumes, each based on related career fields from the Department of Labor's career clusters. Within each volume approximately 10 careers are profiled, encouraging readers to focus on a wide selection of job possibilities, some of which readers may not even know exist. To enable readers to narrow their choices, each chapter offers a self-assessment quiz that helps answer the question, "Is this career for me?" What's more, each job profile includes an insightful look at what the position involves, highlights of a typical day, insight into the work environment, and an interview with someone on the job.

An essential part of the decision to enter a particular field includes how much additional training is needed. Careers in Demand features opportunities that require no further academic study or training beyond high school as well as those that do. Readers in high school can start prepping for careers immediately through volunteer work, internships, academic classes, technical programs, or career academies. (Currently, for instance, one in four students concentrates on a vocational or technical program.) For each profile, the best ways for high school students to prepare are featured in a "Start Preparing Now" section.

For readers who are called to serve in the armed forces, this decision also provides an opportunity to step into a range of careers. Every branch of the armed forces from the army to the coast guard offers training in areas including administrative, construction, electronics, health care, and protective services. One volume of Careers in Demand for High School Graduates is devoted to careers that can be reached with military training. These range from personnel specialist to aircraft mechanic.

Beyond military options, other entry-level careers provide job seekers with an opportunity to test-drive a career without a huge commitment. Compare the ease of switching from being a bank teller to a sales represen-

▲ If you enjoy making things grow, a nursery/greenhouse assistant job could be right for you.

tative, for instance, with that of investing three years and tens of thousands of dollars into a law school education, only to discover a dislike for the profession. Careers in Demand offers not only a look at related careers but also ways to advance in the field. Another section, "Finding a Job," provides job-hunting tips specific to each career. This includes, for instance, advice for teacher assistants to develop a portfolio of their work. As it turns out, employers of entry-level workers aren't looking for degrees and academic achievements. They want employability skills: a sense of responsibility, a willingness to learn, discipline, flexibility, and above all, enthusiasm. Luckily, with 100 jobs profiled in Careers in Demand for High School Graduates, finding the perfect one to get enthusiastic about is easier than ever.

Farmworker

1

Work anywhere there are farms. Find work with ease.
Be essential to the food supply.

WORDS TO UNDERSTAND

agrochemicals: any of a variety of chemicals used to grow food, including pesticides and fertilizers.

consolidation: here, two or more companies combine into one.

thresher: a machine that separates grain or seeds from a crop.

Do you ever look at the produce in your local supermarket and wonder where it comes from? Most of us take it for granted that fresh fruits and vegetables appear on our local store shelves year round as if by magic. But in fact, a tremendous amount of effort goes into planting, growing, picking, packing, and shipping every single apple, spinach leaf, strawberry, and grape. Farmworkers spend all day in fields, their work changing with the seasons as they plant seeds, fertilize them, irrigate them, then help them grow by using **agrochemicals** to keep pests away. When the fruit or vegetable is ready to make the trip to your local supermarket, farmworkers harvest it and prepare it for transport on trucks and airplanes. The work is very hard, and the pay is low, but jobs are always available. With immigration and health care reform topping the political agenda in 2017, the essential role of undocumented immigrants in the national economy—many of whom work in farm labor—has entered mainstream discourse.

◀ Fruits and vegetables may be locally grown, like these for sale in a farmer's market, or they may come from larger farms from the other side of the country. The one thing they have in common are the farmworkers who plant and maintain the crops every day.

Is This Job Right for You?

To find out if being a farmworker is a good fit for you, read each of the following statements and answer "Yes" or "No."

Yes	*No*	**1.** *Do you mind working outdoors in hot weather?*
Yes	*No*	**2.** *Can you be careful in working with farm chemicals?*
Yes	*No*	**3.** *Can you begin working at the minimum wage?*
Yes	*No*	**4.** *Is it okay with you for your work to vary seasonally?*
Yes	*No*	**5.** *Is it important to you that your work is easy to get?*
Yes	*No*	**6.** *Do you speak Spanish, or are you willing to learn?*
Yes	*No*	**7.** *Is it okay that your job does not come with benefits?*
Yes	*No*	**8.** *Do you prefer working outside with your hands more than being inside an office or factory?*
Yes	*No*	**9.** *Can you carefully handle delicate, ripening fruit?*
Yes	*No*	**10.** *Do you like the idea of helping things grow?*

If you can answer "Yes" to most of these questions, read on to find out more about a career as a farmworker.

What's the Work Like?

Farmworkers play a crucial role in ensuring that your local supermarket can stock fresh fruits and vegetables. Food grown and harvested by farmworkers also finds its way into restaurant kitchens and prepared foods. Your work in this field will depend upon the type of crop that you grow and the climate in which you live. The duties of a farmworker who tends orange groves in Florida will differ from those of a farmworker who grows potatoes in Idaho.

There are certain features of the job that are consistent across

TALKING MONEY

Agricultural work is very low paying. The average hourly rate for farmworkers in 2016 was $10.83 per hour. Farmworkers are rarely unionized, and jobs rarely come with benefits, such as health insurance and retirement savings accounts. Jobs in rural areas tend to come with housing; jobs near urban areas are less likely to offer housing as part of the compensation package.

▲ Farmworkers harvest crops in different ways. Some will pick by hand while others will use large machinery.

regions and crops. The work is always seasonal and cyclical and requires a lot of stamina. Whatever the crop being sown, the soil must usually be tilled first, the fruit or vegetable planted, the field irrigated and fertilized, and the crop tended carefully to eradicate weeds and pests. It is a lot of work! Most farmworkers start their workday at sunrise and finish at sunset in order to take advantage of all available daylight. This means that you will be traveling to and from work in darkness. Employers differ in the accommodations they offer workers, so seek one that provides access to food, water, shelter from the elements, and bathroom facilities. Farmworkers must take precautions to avoid both sunburn and sunstroke. In early spring or autumn, cold, wind, and rain can also be factors in your day.

As noted above, the work of farmworkers changes with the growing cycle of the crop. Harvesting is usually the busiest time, when you may be asked to put in extra hours to be sure all of the crop is picked and packed for shipping at the appropriate point of ripeness. Harvesting of delicate fruits is still done by hand, but certain crops are harvested by machines. You might be taught how to drive a tractor and how to use farm equipment like a **thresher**, skills that can be essential to your future advancement. Most likely you will work on a crew that will function like an assembly line, with each worker having a specific

▲ Large threshers, like this one, are used to harvest wheat, which will then be used to make breads and cereals.

function in the process of picking, packing, and loading the produce in the field. As you gain experience and demonstrate responsibility, you may get to move up to be a driver or crew leader.

Who's Hiring?

- Farm labor contractors

- Large, agribusiness companies

- Small farms

- Orchards

- Vineyards

Learn more about working on different types of farms.

Where Are the Jobs?

Farm work is seasonal, with planting and harvesting the busiest times of year. The work is, obviously, mostly outdoors in fields, orchards, or vineyards. Long hours and six- or seven-day workweeks are common during planting and harvesting seasons. Farmworkers are outside for many hours in all kinds of weather. The sun can be especially hard to deal with, but there also may be cold, wind, and rain. Working during all of the daylight hours may mean commuting to and from work in the dark. During the workday, there may be limited access to water, food, shelter, and bathroom facilities.

Since farm work is seasonal, you may need to obtain alternative employment in the off-season. Some farmworkers, called migrant workers, move to new locations as crops ripen or to begin a growing season. This unsettled lifestyle is sometimes temporarily enjoyable to younger workers. Some jobs come with bunk-style shared housing, but some jobs do not provide accommodation. It depends, in part, on the size of the agricultural operation and the distance to suitable housing for the workers.

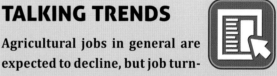

TALKING TRENDS

Agricultural jobs in general are expected to decline, but job turnover is high and opportunities should prove readily available for the foreseeable future. Consolidation of farms, technical advances in farm equipment, and trade agreements with foreign countries are mainly responsible for the projected decline in overall jobs. However, jobs are expected to open up as consumers turn increasingly to farmers' markets and local businesses when buying produce. Farmworkers are increasingly likely to be employed by farm labor contractors rather than being directly hired by the farms themselves.

A Typical Day

Here are the highlights for a typical day for a farmworker on a large agribusiness farm during harvest season.

Get up before dawn. Because most agricultural work is performed outdoors, laborers rely on natural light to see what they are doing. In order to take advantage of all the daylight in the fields, it is necessary to travel to work while it is still dark.

NOTES FROM THE FIELD

Farmer, Litchfield, Maine

Q: *How did you get your job?*

A: I grew up in the middle of a large city. I hated it. I always wanted horses and cows. When I was young, my parents, brother, and I would go out to buy sweet corn every summer Sunday after church at a local dairy farm. The first place I went was to the barn to play with the calves and pat the cows. Later on the nephew of the farmers became a veterinarian and raised racing quarter horses. I got to visit both the horses and the cows! I was in heaven.

I got a job when I turned sixteen and saved enough money to buy my first horse, which I supported. I became an apprentice horse trainer and learned horse breeding and raising. . . . I met my husband to be when I boarded my horses at his stable. He had the same dream . . . a dairy farm. Since dairying was almost impossible to get into in Massachusetts at the time, we moved to Maine with our two young sons. We finally got our dairy farm. I had a herd of dairy goats as well as dairy cattle and did well with milk production from both animals.

We set up the cattle milk machines to accommodate the goats and mixed the goat milk in with the cows' milk. We started getting a premium price for it because the protein and butter fat went up and the bacteria count went down. Only our sales rep knew we had the goats' milk piped in with the cows' milk.

I still have horses and goats. My horses are used mostly as pasture pets these days, but I still raise the goats. I have four dairy goats left from the original herd, but I have since added Boer goats to the mix. Boer goats are meat goats, and goat meat, or *chevon*, is becoming popular due to its low fat–low cholesterol content. I still milk the dairy goats, but, instead of selling the milk, I make cheese, soap, butter, pudding, custard, and lotions from what milk I don't use in the house for drinking. I sell the male kids for meat, and a very select group of buck kids for breeding. The doe kids are either kept as replacements or sold for breeding. I have a full time job to support my livestock hobby, but the kid and soap sales help pay the feed bill. I am a small farm now, but I still run it like I did the big farm years ago.

Q: *What do you like best about your job?*

A: I feel at peace when I am with my animals. I have rheumatoid arthritis, so the work keeps my joints limber. I get a real good feeling when an animal I have bred wins at shows or produces a record amount of milk. After being at work all day, the down time I have with my animals is a great stress reliever.

Q: *What's the most challenging part of your job?*

A: As with any type of farming, making a living is the biggest challenge. Milk and livestock prices are very low, while the price of feed, fuel, supplies, veterinary care . . . the normal day-to-day business costs . . . continue to rise. Only farms that have been in the family and are paid off can make a living.

Q: *What are the keys to success for being a farmworker?*

A: Four keys to success . . . hard work, long hours is the biggest key. Getting higher education at an agricultural college will help the business end as well as the animal husbandry part. Being able to run the farm as a business while still realizing that you are dealing with live animals is a major issue. You must learn to think with your brain and not let your heart rule the business. I had a hard time with culling. I still do. I get attached to my animals. . . . Some of them end up being shipped to slaughter; it's a fact of life. If you can't deal with it, then farming may not be for you.

Fill containers with produce. Containers that are appropriate for whatever fruit or vegetable you are picking will be provided at the end of every row in the field. It may be part of your job to load the empty containers onto a truck and drive them to the field, or you and the other workers may ride on the truck with the containers out to the place where you stopped picking the previous day.

Load containers for transport. When darkness falls, you will be forced by lack of light to leave the fields and pack up the produce that you have picked so it can be shipped to packaging and distribution centers. This part of your job may involve heavy lifting or—increasingly as technology advances and farming becomes more automated—it may involve operating equipment that packs and stacks produce for transport.

▲ As a farmworker, you will learn how to operate heavy machinery like combines and tractors.

Start Preparing Now

• Look up information on agriculture-related careers on the Internet or at your local library. There are some careers that you might find more lucrative or appealing than that of farmworker but they may require education beyond the high school level.

• Look for summer jobs as a farmworker. The job does not require a high school degree so there is nothing stopping you from getting a job during summer vacation while you are still in school.

• Begin studying Spanish, if you do not already speak it.

Training and How to Get It

No previous education or training is needed to obtain a job as a farmworker. It is one of the least-skilled jobs available, which is one reason it appeals to immigrants, both legal and illegal, who lack English language skills and, in some cases, lack any formal education. All of the training you will need can be obtained on the job. This includes any equipment that you may have to operate. There isn't really any place to learn to use farm equipment except on a farm!

Learn the Lingo

Here are a few terms of the trade:

- **Combine** A machine, either self-propelled or drawn by a tractor, that cuts, threshes, and cleans a standing crop, such as grains or beans.

- **Crop rotation** The practice of growing different crops on the same land from year to year to helps preserve the nutrients in the soil.

- **Power take-off (PTO)** A shaft on the rear of a tractor that is driven by the tractor's motor. It supplies rotative power to attachments such as balers, mowers, and combines.

Finding a Job

The best part of being a farmworker is the ease of finding employment. During planting and harvest season, there are usually plenty of jobs, and farmers and agribusinesses often complain that they have more work than workers. Since many farmworkers do not speak English, look for advertisements for farm laborers in Spanish-language publications. You can ask farms if they are hiring directly—particularly small, organic farms that are becoming increasingly popular with consumers. That said, many workers are employed by farm labor contractors; these contractors will provide workers to different farms on an as-needed basis.

Tips for Success

- Love your work. What you don't get in salary and benefits or upward mobility you need to find in satisfaction in working with your hands on the land, growing the food we eat.

- Follow directions and be prompt and responsible.

Reality Check

Farm work is a low-paid profession. The work is often physically demanding, subject to the vagaries of weather, and only seasonally available. There may be health concerns due to constant chemical exposure. There is an appeal to working outdoors, on the land, but think seriously about the trade-offs involved in salary, work environment, and stability.

Related Jobs to Consider

Grounds maintenance worker. These laborers look after the landscaping in a variety of settings. The work is not highly skilled or highly paid, but it varies seasonally, and you could work at college campuses, golf courses, sports facilities, corporate office complexes, malls, schools, parks, private homes, and anyplace else with landscaping that must be trimmed, planted, watered, and otherwise maintained.

LEARN MORE ONLINE

NATIONAL FFA ORGANIZATION
This site provides information about education and jobs in the agricultural sciences. http://www.ffa.org

NATIONAL FARMWORKER JOBS PROGRAM
Site run by the U.S. Department of Labor that provides information to help unemployed and underemployed farmworkers achieve economic self-sufficiency. https://www.doleta.gov/Farmworker/

U.S. DEPARTMENT OF AGRICULTURE
The USDA Web site provides general information about agricultural developments, regulations, and employment. http://www.usda.gov/wps/portal/usdahome

Nursery or greenhouse worker. Employees of a commercial nursery grow plants that will be purchased and transplanted. They care for seedlings, prune and fertilize young plants, and advise customers on which plants to choose for their growing environment.

Livestock farmworker. A livestock farmworker is a similar type of agricultural worker, but instead of caring for crops you would be caring for chickens, cattle, pigs, or other animals that are raised for human consumption.

How to Move Up

- If you prove yourself to be a competent and reliable worker, and if you have good communication skills, you might advance to a supervisory position, such as crew leader. It will be an asset if you can speak Spanish.

- To move beyond the level of farmworker or labor supervisor, you are likely to need a degree in agricultural science or farm management. With such a degree in hand, you could become a farm manager.

- Related jobs that you could aspire to include professions such as purchasing agents for farms or farm-products companies, or you might become a farmer yourself.

TEXT-DEPENDENT QUESTIONS

1. *What is the average hourly pay for farmworkers?*

2. *What is a typical day like?*

3. *What are some related jobs you might consider?*

RESEARCH PROJECTS

1. *Knowing a bit of Spanish will get you far and may even be a requirement on large farms. If you are not already studying the language, you can start learning for free with apps like Duolingo or busuu.*

2. *Try growing some food on your own. If you have a yard, you might be able to start a small plot there. But if not, container gardening is still a great option. For help getting started, check out sites like The Old Farmer's Almanac (https://www.almanac.com/content/container-gardening-vegetables) and Gardener's Supply Company (https://www.gardeners.com/how-to/urban-gardening-with-vegetables/5491.html).*

Livestock Farmworker

2

*Make working with live animals your living.
Nurture the next generation of food. Be outstanding
in your field.*

WORDS TO UNDERSTAND

aquaculture: raising fish and/or aquatic plants for food.

depleted: used up.

feedlot: a location (could be an open area or a building) where farm animals are fed.

milking parlor: a room or barn reserved for the mechanical milking of cows.

Have you eaten a hamburger recently? How about a turkey sandwich or a piece of fried chicken? Before that beef or poultry ended up on your plate, it was an animal that was bred for food, probably raised on a diet designed to bulk it up quickly, slaughtered, then processed and packaged and shipped to the local store or restaurant where you bought it. It's a long way from a steer grazing in a field to a ground sirloin patty sizzling on your grill. Someone has to care for animals that are raised for food. The job of a livestock farmworker is hard, but many jobs are available in this traditional field.

◀ Animals need to be fed and cared for seven days a week, 365 days a year.

Is This Job Right for You?

To find out if being a livestock farmworker is a good fit for you, read each of the following statements and answer "Yes" or "No."

Yes	No	1.	*Can you tolerate being around animals that are being raised for meat?*
Yes	No	2.	*Do you not mind getting wet and dirty on the job?*
Yes	No	3.	*Are you willing to do physical labor all day for your work?*
Yes	No	4.	*Do you accept that the farm animals you work with sometimes may be difficult to manage?*
Yes	No	5.	*Can you tolerate concentrated smells of animal excrement?*
Yes	No	6.	*Can you tolerate being on your feet all day and doing some heavy lifting?*
Yes	No	7.	*Can you exercise caution in the use of hazardous machinery and equipment?*
Yes	No	8.	*Are you capable of participating in animal-management activities such as branding, castrating, and debeaking?*
Yes	No	9.	*Can you listen to and follow directions?*
Yes	No	10.	*Do you have good coordination and balance?*

If you can answer "Yes" to most of these questions, read on to find out more about a career in the livestock industry.

What's the Work Like?

A livestock farmworker's tasks depend upon the type of animals that are being raised. Animals commonly raised for food include poultry (including eggs), cattle, sheep, pigs, and fish. There are even bee farms that produce honey. As you can imagine, the work you'd perform on a fish farm is considerably different from what you'd do on a cattle ranch.

Even with the same type of animal, the work varies by the purpose for which they are being raised. Cattle, for example, are raised for beef and also for veal and milk. Cattle raised for beef are kept in **feedlots**

TALKING MONEY

The average hourly rate for livestock laborers in 2016 was $12.90 per hour. Livestock laborers are rarely unionized, and the jobs tend to lack benefits.

or in pastures where they graze. Out West, they often graze on rangeland instead of in fenced pastures. Usually, if they are grass-fed at all, it is not for their entire lives. Most spend some time before slaughter fattening up in feedlots, where they are fed crops that are grown for this purpose. The care of beef cattle resembles the classic cowboy image, except that technology has changed how most of the work is performed. Instead of riding on horseback to patrol the fence line and make any necessary repairs, today you would be driving a truck loaded with equipment for repairs and maintenance. You still have to herd the cattle, driving them from one pasture to another as seasons change and grass gets **depleted**, but, again, you are likely to do this with GPS (Global Positioning System)-equipped vehicles—including helicopters—rather than on horseback, and getting cattle to move where you want them to go is more likely to involve an electric cattle prod than a herding dog. Calves are still castrated, branded, vaccinated, and given antibiotics and other drugs, but the process is highly mechanized now. The work is still performed outdoors in all weather, and it is still seasonal, but it is less labor-intensive nowadays.

▲ Cattle in pastures have to be herded to different feeding areas with the change of seasons.

Now let's contrast that work environment with a dairy farm. Dairy cows must be milked twice a day. This process is also highly mechanized today, with **milking parlors** that feature milking machines that do the milking for you. But the cows still need to be brought in from their pasture twice a day, and there is a seasonal cycle of breeding, pregnancy, and calving on the farm. Cows and calves often get sick and need special care, and the milking parlor and equipment must be thoroughly cleaned and disinfected after each milking. The work is repetitive and time-consuming. It also takes place outdoors in all weather, and is seasonal in nature, but there is an indoor component of it due to the milking parlor.

Poultry and egg farms tend to be the quintessential "factory farms" where chickens are debeaked and given antibiotics so they can live packed into tiny cages without harming one another from the stress or succumbing to infections. Sometimes hundreds of thousands of chickens are packed into one building. The work here involves feeding and cleaning, but the

▲ Even though milking parlors have made the milking process easier, livestock farmers are still needed to attach the devices to the cows' udders in order to extract milk.

▲ The eggs produced on a large farm are processed on a conveyor belt for easy sorting.

cages are arranged in such a way that even this process is highly mechanized. On most large egg farms, eggs tumble down a chute onto a conveyor belt where they are cleaned, sorted, and packaged by machine, not by workers.

However, the fastest-growing segment of the food market is for organic products—especially milk and eggs. The systems of production for these products often include a concern for animal welfare. Because their produce would lose its premium price if they were administered the various drugs given to most farm animals, creatures in the organic chain must be treated well so they don't become diseased. Farms in the organics marketplace vary in how they treat their workers, but many place a similar value on the conditions for both workers and animals.

See what it's like to work on a dairy farm.

The work in **aquaculture** is quite different from the type of labor involved in raising land animals. You might be stocking ponds, feeding fish stocks, and managing nets and water filtration systems, as well as harvesting and packaging fish and other aquatic life.

Who's Hiring?

- Factory farms raising poultry, cattle, or pigs

- Egg and poultry farms

- Pig farms

- Beef cattle ranches

- Dairy farms

- Fish farms (aquaculture)

- Apiaries (bee farms)

Where Are the Jobs?

If you work with large animals like cattle, you are likely to spend most if not all of your time outdoors. Beef cattle ranches tend to be found in the Southwest and West. Feedlots tend to be more numerous in the Plains states. Dairy farms, which involve some indoor work in the milking parlor, are concentrated in the East and Midwest but can be found almost everywhere. Hog farms are found all over but are more numerous in the Southeast and the Plains states. Poultry and egg farms are fairly evenly distributed around the country, as are apiaries. Aquaculture is concentrated near the coasts, particularly the Pacific Northwest. Wherever you live, some type of animal is raised for food near you.

Agricultural workers tend to work longer hours than workers in other fields. Animals need to be fed and cared for seven days a week, including holidays. This may mean that you

NOTES FROM THE FIELD

Livestock farmworker, Bremen, Ohio

Q: *How did you get your job?*

A: I acquired my job while in FFA (Future Farmers of America). The client called in, and it was assigned to me. FFA is a very educational program if you are wanting to work in the farm industry.

Q: *What do you like best about your job?*

A: What I like best about my job is feeding the calves their milk out of bottles in the morning and afternoon. They solely depend on you; I would say that they think of you as their mother.

Q: *What's the most challenging part of your job?*

A: The most challenging parts of my job are getting up at 3:30 in the morning and the continuous repetition.

Q: *What are the keys to success for being a livestock farmworker?*

A: I would say that the most important keys to success in this industry are loving what you do and truly caring about your animals. It takes a lot of drive and motivation to get up early every day and do the same thing over and over again.

work in shifts. Unlike crops, animals need care year round, but the work is still seasonal in nature. Spring is a busy time with calving and lambing. There are also particular times of year when castrating, branding, vaccinating, and slaughtering take place.

A Typical Day

Here are the highlights for a typical day for a livestock farmworker on a dairy farm.

Bring cows into the milking parlor. Cows are creatures of habit, and they are usually lined up at the gate at the proper time. There will be a series of chutes directing them into a line for the milking machines. The rows are raised so that you do not need to bend over to hook the machines up to the udders.

Clean the milking parlor. Strict regulations govern the sanitation of milking parlors. You will need to thoroughly spray and scrub the facility after each use. You will also need to clean the milk tanks after they are emptied into trucks as well as monitor the temperature and bacterial contamination in the tanks. You will also track milk production per cow so that low-producing cows can be culled and the offspring of particularly high-producing cows can be kept to strengthen the herd.

Bring the cows in again. The cows need to be milked twice a day, so the whole cycle repeats.

Start Preparing Now

- If you live in a rural area, join the local 4-H club and take agricultural science classes at your high school. If you live in the city, these courses and clubs might not be as accessible to you, but see if there is anything within commuting distance.

- Learn all you can about the livestock industry. Read and watch videos about life on various types of farms. Visit local farms, if you can. This will help you decide which animal and lifestyle are right for you.

- Look for summer jobs on local farms. Since there are no educational requirements for this work, you can get a job while you are still in school. There are certain laws restricting work that is considered dangerous to those over 18, but some jobs will be open to you.

Training and How to Get It

Most agricultural workers, including livestock farmworkers, do not have high school diplomas. The lack of formal qualifications or experience required for the job attracts immigrants, both legal and illegal, who lack English language skills. Most jobs offer on-the-job training. The more factory-like and mechanized the work, the less a potential employer is going to care about skills or experience. The one sector of the industry where experience may be a factor is beef cattle ranching. A ranch manager is likely to favor applicants who have had some experience handling cattle. Also, some high-end and smaller farms may look for applicants who have taken agricultural science classes. This is particularly true on breeding farms.

Learn the Lingo

Here are a few terms of the trade:

- **Steer** Castrated bull calf, usually raised for beef.

- **Animal unit (AU)** A unit for measuring feed consumption and animal density on farms. One animal unit is usually equivalent to 1,000 pounds or about one mature cow.

- **Freshen** A fresh cow has just given birth and is beginning a lactation cycle.

Finding a Job

To find a job, approach farms in your area and ask if they are hiring. Advertisements for jobs might appear in local papers. Look at Spanish-language publications, since many farmworkers are native Spanish speakers. There are some independent recruiters who fill job openings for large operations, such as factory poultry farms. If there are recruiters in your area, register with them, and they will alert you to job openings. There are some online job sites that list agricultural jobs, but most jobs advertised online are likely to be higher-level managerial or inspection/compliance-related jobs that require special training, certification, or experience. Your best bet is to ask directly at local farms. There is a high turnover rate in agricultural jobs, so there are frequently entry-level openings. Keep checking at the same farms until vacancies arise. You have a better chance of getting hired if you are flexible about your hours and exhibit a willingness to work less desirable shifts.

Tips for Success

- Have a high tolerance for routine. Animals, as living creatures with minds of their own, can be unpredictable. This will provide some variety in your workday. Yet the overriding characteristic of life on a factory farm is the routine. The animals are kept on a strict schedule, designed to maximize productivity, and this means repetition for the workers who care for them.

- Stay focused while working; with big animals and heavy equipment, small mistakes can prove costly!

Reality Check

The cowboy is a bygone figure of the American landscape. Livestock farmworkers are in the business of food production, and in this industry animals are seen as economic units of production.

Related Jobs to Consider

Animal caretaker. Animal caretakers work in shelters that house unwanted or stray animals. They keep records, feed, clean cages, test animals for temperament, obtain veterinary care for sick or injured animals, and assist in euthanizing unwanted animals. They also may deal directly with the public, facilitating adoptions and screening potential adopters. Animal caretakers also work in boarding kennels and doggy daycare facilities.

LEARN MORE ONLINE

NATIONAL FFA ORGANIZATION
This site provides information about education and jobs in the agricultural sciences. http://www.ffa.org

NATIONAL FARMWORKER JOBS PROGRAM
Site run by the U.S. Department of Labor that provides information to help migrant and underemployed farmworkers achieve economic self-sufficiency. https://www.doleta.gov/Farmworker/

U.S. DEPARTMENT OF AGRICULTURE
The USDA Web site provides general information about agricultural developments, regulations and employment. https://www.usda.gov/

Groom. Grooms care for riding and driving horses in stables. They feed their charges, cool them off and rub them down after exercise, bathe them, and make them look presentable for shows or other appearances. They also care for all of the tack (equipment, such as saddles and harnesses) that the horses use. Of course, they also clean stalls!

Butcher, slaughterer, or meatpacker. Butchering and related occupations are the next step in the process of turning the steer that the livestock farmworker raises into hamburger for the table. Animals are shipped from farms to slaughterhouses, where they are killed, chopped up, and packaged.

How to Move Up

- If you prove yourself to be a competent and reliable worker, you may move up to a supervisory role.

- If you would like to become a farm manager or a specialist in an area such as breeding or inspecting livestock, you will need to pursue further education and training. See if a local college offers an associate's or bachelor's degree in agricultural science. In most degree programs, you can specialize in a certain area, such as breeding or inspection. The FFA Web site provides useful information about educational options. Ask your employer what additional education you would need to move up to a position that interests you.

TEXT-DEPENDENT QUESTIONS

1. *What is aquaculture?*

2. *What are some of the different types of farms that raise livestock?*

3. *What kind of training might you need to move up in this field?*

RESEARCH PROJECTS

1. *Find a working farm in your area; if you don't know of one, try searching online for "farm" and your town. Visit the farm and talk to the people there about what they do. Many farms offer tours at particular times.*

2. *Find out more about the raising of farm animals in these books:* The Art and Science of Grazing *by Sarah Flack;* How to Speak Chicken *by Melissa Caughey; and* The Inner World of Farm Animals *by Amy Hatkoff. Your school librarian may have additional suggestions.*

Pest Control Technician, Animal Control Officer

Rescue abused and neglected animals. Work with common and exotic animals. Rid houses of unwanted pests.

WORDS TO UNDERSTAND

eradicate: to completely eliminate something.

impound: here, describes taking custody of an animal whose owner is unknown or has mistreated it.

resurgence: revival.

unsocialized: here, describes an animal that does not behave well with humans or sometimes even with other animals.

This chapter covers two jobs that are actually quite different. They are featured together because they both involve the issue of humans and animals living side by side in the modern world. Wild animals and insects sometimes settle in people's houses and cause problems, ranging from just a nuisance to serious health and structural issues. Pest control technicians **eradicate** insects, vermin, and wild animals that have taken up residence in buildings. Domestic animals like cats and dogs sometimes escape or are abandoned by their owners and need to be taken off the streets so that they do not get hurt or killed, and so they do not pose a threat to people

◀ When exterminating insects and other pests, workers wear special gear to protect them from harmful chemicals.

and other animals. Unfortunately, pets are also sometimes abused or neglected by their owners and need to be rescued from a bad situation. Animal control officers (ACOs) handle this important job.

Is This Job Right for You?

To find out if being a pest control technician or animal control officer is a good fit for you, read each of the following statements and answer "Yes" or "No."

Yes	*No*	**1.**	*Do you love animals and hate to see them abused or neglected?*
Yes	*No*	**2.**	*Can you accept the risks associated with working with strange animals that might be frightened, injured, or **unsocialized**?*
Yes	*No*	**3.**	*Can you deal with people who may be hostile?*
Yes	*No*	**4.**	*Does educating people about proper care for their animals appeal to you?*
Yes	*No*	**5.**	*Are you observant and detail oriented?*
Yes	*No*	**6.**	*Can prepare reports and take photographs that may be used in prosecution of cases of cruelty and neglect?*
Yes	*No*	**7.**	*Are you prepared to crawl into basements, attics, and other dirty and inaccessible spaces as a regular part of your job?*
Yes	*No*	**8.**	*Could you manage any phobias you might have of insects, rodents, or snakes?*
Yes	*No*	**9.**	*Would you enjoy educating people about ways to keep their homes free of pests?*
Yes	*No*	**10.**	*Can you use the necessary care to work with pesticides and other chemicals on a regular basis?*

If you can answer "Yes" to most of these questions, read on to find out more about a career in the fields of pest management or animal control.

What's the Work Like?

An ACO enforces city and state animal welfare laws. She or he investigates reported cases of animal cruelty or neglect and has the authority to impound animals, issue citations, and make arrests. Conducting inspections and issuing permits are also part the of the ACO's responsibilities. There is a lot of paperwork involved in this job. An ACO must keep accurate records and prepare reports on all cases, including taking photographs of neglected and abused animals and the conditions in which they were living. The successful prosecution of animal abusers depends upon how well the ACO documents the cases.

Education is also part of an ACO's duties. When an ACO investigates cases of neglect, instead of arresting the offender sometimes the ACO will issue a warning and educate the person about proper care for animals. The ACO will then make follow-up visits to ensure compliance. This strategy can be effective

▲ Unfortunately, there are many animals that are abused and kept in unhealthy conditions. An animal control officer (ACO) will remove these animals and help to find them a better home.

for offenders who are not being deliberately cruel or neglectful but who are genuinely ignorant of their animals' needs.

A pest control technician will travel to buildings and nearby areas that are infested with some type of pest and attempt to eradicate it. In some cases, the pest control technician may have to identify the species of pest and find creative ways of repelling pests when conventional techniques fail. Gaining access to areas that pests inhabit may be challenging. Climbing, crawling, and squeezing into small spaces are regular features of the job.

Once the pest has been located and identified, the pest control technician has a variety of methods to eliminate it. In some cases, chemical pesticides are used. Due to their certification, pest control technicians have access to regulated chemicals that are restricted from use by the general public. The safe use of these chemicals requires equipment, including respirators, that can be heavy and hot to wear. But pesticides are not the only option for eradicating pests. The use of a combination of pest control techniques, called Integrated Pest Management (IPM), is increasingly popular and considered safer and more effective than the use of pesticides alone.

Who's Hiring?

- City law enforcement agencies

- Counties

- Privately run humane societies with local government contracts

- Pest management companies

Where Are the Jobs?

As an animal control officer, your job environment will depend upon whether you are based in an urban or rural area. In an urban area, you will be driving an official law enforcement vehicle, and your day will consist of driving around to houses and apartment complexes to investigate complaints and conduct follow-up visits to ensure compliance. You may have to go into dangerous neighborhoods to pursue cases of cruelty and neglect as well as investigate dog- or cockfighting rings. You will have to do a lot of driving to follow up on reports of stray dogs, wildlife coming into urban areas, or rabid animals. In rural areas, your calls are more likely to involve larger animals, such as horses, and you may have to drive longer distances to get out to farms. You will also spend part of your time at animal shelters, where you will drop off animals that are being **impounded**, photograph them, and follow up on their progress. You may use this information when you are called to present evidence in court, another important facet of your job.

A pest control technician works for a company that responds to calls from clients, members of the public with an animal-related problem. As a technician, you are likely to spend much of your time in your company's truck or van, driving to job sites. Depending on the population density of your area, you may be called mainly to houses or primarily to apartment or commercial buildings. The types of pests that you will confront will also vary considerably by geographic location. One type of pest that is making a **resurgence** everywhere is bedbugs. You are likely to encounter them wherever you work.

TALKING TRENDS

Animal control is a stressful and demanding job, but it is a career that inspires dedication, so turnover is not as high as in other high-stress animal care occupations, such as shelter work. As pet ownership increases, job opportunities are likely to increase in this and related fields.

Job prospects are likely to be good for pest control technicians for several reasons. The occupation is generally considered unappealing, which means that demand for workers is usually higher than supply. The job—unlike that of ACO—has a high turnover rate, leading to continual job openings. Also, as the population becomes more affluent and the standard of living increases, demand will be higher for professional pest control. The population is also shifting toward the Sunbelt, the area of the country most prone to pests, and meanwhile a gradual warming of the climate is likely to encourage pest population growth.

A Typical Day

Here are the highlights for a typical day for an animal control officer employed by a medium-sized city.

Follow up on previous calls. If you have no urgent new calls, you may begin your workday by driving around to see if owners who have been ordered to take better care of their pets are doing so. You will check for adequate food, water, and shelter and a safe environment free of hazards, and you will assess the overall condition of the animals. You must record everything that you see. If you discover noncompliance, you may end up impounding animals from the site.

▲ Pest control experts may have to fumigate entire homes or businesses in order to rid them of bedbugs such as this one.

Attend to the day's schedule of calls. When someone calls animal control to report a suspected case of abuse or a stray animal in the area, you will get a call on your radio with an address to go to. If there are more calls than you can cover in one day, you may start each workday with a list of calls to make as you can get to them.

Accurately and thoroughly record your findings for the day. Keeping accurate records is an important part of your job. It could mean the difference between an animal dying or being rescued, and successful prosecution of abuse cases depends upon detailed written and photographic evidence.

Start Preparing Now

- Applicants for animal control jobs are usually required to demonstrate at least a year of experience in animal care. Look for a summer job assisting in a shelter, grooming salon, boarding kennel, or veterinarian's office. Most of these places hire high school students to clean kennels and assist with other menial tasks. This experience could mean the difference between getting a job or not being chosen.

- If you aspire to be a pest control technician, it will be to your benefit to take chemistry and math classes in high school.

- Both of these jobs require considerable driving, and applicants without a clean driving record are usually automatically disqualified from consideration. Make sure your driving record is clean and stays clean.

Training and How to Get It

Since animal control is a branch of law enforcement, applicants have to face many of the same hurdles as police academy recruits. There is usually a physical abilities test that assesses flexibility, agility, and physical strength. A medical examination is often required, and this will include a psychological screening—including a personality inventory evaluation. A comprehensive background check is required, along with a written test. These usually must be successfully passed before the candidate moves on to other areas of screening. New recruits undergo a lengthy probationary period of on-the-job training where they accompany an experienced ACO on calls. Many of these requirements are waived in rural or less affluent areas that have a part-time ACO.

 See what it's like to be an ACO.

The training and certification required to become a pest control technician are extensive, but the good news is that you can complete much of it on the job—often at your employer's expense. As a new hire, you will be classified as an apprentice technician. You will have to complete general training in safe pesticide handling and use before you will be allowed to perform any pest control services for clients. In addition to the general training, you will need to attend training in specific types of pest control, such as termite abatement, rodent control, and fumigation. Training requirements vary by state but usually involve at least 60 hours on the job and 10 hours of specific training for each category. Once apprentices have completed this basic training, they can assist licensed applicators in performing pest control services under supervision. After obtaining additional education and experience, apprentices can take an examination to become certified applicators. Most states

NOTES FROM THE FIELD

Animal control officer, Denmark, Maine

Q: *How did you get your job?*

A: I was retired after selling my business. My wife, Marilyn, and I raised dogs, and I had been brought up with horses. The local chief of police asked me if I would help out with animal control. I got certified and became an animal control officer (ACO). Soon I was doing the same in nine other towns, so I was covering ten towns in western Maine.

Q: *What do you like best about your job?*

A: The thing I like best about this work is that each day I have a score or report card that allows me to honestly know and feel good about the fact that I have done something to improve the existence of at least one or maybe several animals. Most of the times the animals involved are dogs, cats, horses, and sometimes other types of farm animals. The way we help is to make sure all the animals in our area are kept and cared for as the law requires. It is very satisfying to cause an improvement in the environmental conditions of the animals and also to help educate the owners or keepers as to how they can do better. It is also satisfying to charge the owners or keepers that continuously ignore the requirements and show beyond a doubt that they do not care about the law and even worse about their animals.

Q: *What's the most challenging part of your job?*

A: The most challenging part is to make sure to stay in touch with all methods of handling all the types of animals. You must keep yourself and your staff educated and up to date on animal handling. This is for the safety of the handlers and the animals. An equally challenging facet of the job is to control your emotions, actions, and attitudes toward the people involved in animal cases. Sometimes the first things that are evident as you arrive on a scene are enough to possibly make it very difficult to investigate thoroughly and effectively. Handle all with respect, politeness, and fairness, and show a professional knowledge.

Q: *What are the keys to success to being an animal control officer?*

A: The key to success in animal control is to approach every thing from the point of view of the animal. You are the *only* voice that animal has! If you can do this you will feel as I do: Why haven't I done this all my life?

require that applicators attend continuing education and take additional examinations to be recertified at intervals of one or more years.

Learn the Lingo

Here are a few terms of the trade:

- **Integrated pest management (IPM)** An increasingly popular method of pest control that relies on safer and more environmentally friendly means than pesticides, including natural predators, pest-resistant plants, and other nonchemical methods of discouraging pest infestation.

▲ ACOs use catch poles to safely capture animals.

▲ When entire buildings are fumigated, a large tent is placed around them, sealing off all air space. The chemicals are then able to spread and kill the unwanted pests without harming anyone in the area.

- **Catch pole** Main tool used by ACOs to catch frightened or unsocialized animals. It consists of a metal pole with a noose on the end. When the noose is placed around the animal's neck, the ACO can tighten it via a lever on the pole. It keeps the animal at arm's length to reduce the risk of injury to the handler.

- **Fumigation** A technique for eliminating pests, usually insects, that involves sealing all openings to an area and pumping pesticides into the sealed space. The chemicals used are usually highly toxic so fumigation must be conducted in a conscientious manner, with careful control over when it is safe for humans and pets to reenter the area.

Finding a Job

Since animal control officers are local government employees, you need to check for openings wherever your city or town advertises civil service job vacancies. If you are unsure where to look, call the mayor's office; someone there should be able to direct you to the correct Web site. You may find listings in your local paper, but some municipalities are advertising vacancies exclusively online now. If you live in a rural area, you are more likely to be hired by the county. Look under services in your local telephone book and call the animal control office, which should be able to tell you everything you need to know about finding and applying for vacancies.

Potential pest control technicians can phone local pest control companies directly and ask if they are hiring. Vacancies may also be advertised in local classified job listings.

Tips for Success

- Love, really love, animals. Animal control work is inappropriate for you if you are indifferent to the suffering of the animals whose welfare you are assigned to protect.

- Never cut corners with safety, and stay up to date on newer, less toxic, pest management techniques.

Reality Check

Both animal control and pest management involve job-specific risks. Workers in both professions are at risk from bites and scratches from frightened or rabid animals. Animal control officers face an additional danger from the owners, who often do not take kindly to their animals being impounded or to being told how to take care of them. Pest control technicians are exposed to dangerous chemicals on an ongoing basis, which poses a health risk that only you can decide if you are willing to bear.

Related Jobs to Consider

Animal caretaker. Animal caretakers work in shelters that house unwanted or stray animals. They keep records, feed, clean cages, test animals for temperament, obtain veterinary care for sick or injured animals, and assist in euthanizing unwanted animals. They may also deal directly with the public, facilitating adoptions and screening potential adopters. Animal caretakers also work in boarding kennels and doggy daycare facilities.

Animal trainer. Like animal control officers, animal trainers are involved in teaching pet owners how to properly care for and handle their pets. Trainers often get to work one-on-one with owners and their pets for an extended period and have the satisfaction of seeing progress in overcoming behavioral problems. The increasing popularity of pets has led to recent growth in this gratifying but not very lucrative field.

Building inspector. Building inspectors assess houses and other structures for soundness and safety before they are sold to new owners. Searching for signs of infestation by termites and other pests is one of the main items on a building inspector's checklist.

LEARN MORE ONLINE

NATIONAL ANIMAL CONTROL ASSOCIATION
This site contains information about the training and certification you need to become an animal control officer. It also includes information on jobs and earnings. http://www. nacanet.org

NATIONAL PEST MANAGEMENT ASSOCIATION, INC
This is the national trade organization for the pest control industry. http://www.pestworld.org

How to Move Up

- With additional certifications, training, and experience, animal control officers can sometimes move up to a supervisory role. Upward mobility is dependent upon the size of the jurisdiction. A county with just one ACO cannot really offer a higher-level position. On the other hand, a large municipality is likely to have a hierarchy of animal control staff, with supervisors overseeing other ACOs.

- The pest control industry changes quickly, and just to maintain their job, never mind moving up, pest control technicians need to attend continuing education classes and take periodic examinations to renew and enhance their certifications. One you have several years of experience as a licensed pesticide applicator, you can sit for exams to become a supervisor. These examinations are administered by states, and requirements vary among states.

TEXT-DEPENDENT QUESTIONS

1. *What is a typical day in the life of an ACO?*

2. *What is IPM and why is it important?*

3. *How might you go about looking for a job?*

4. *What are some alternative careers you might consider?*

1. *Find out about animal protection laws and how they vary by state. Search for "animal protection laws" (or "animal cruelty laws") and your own state, then search for several other locations. What do you notice about the laws in different parts of the country? Are some places stricter than others? What aspects remain the same, regardless of location?*

2. *Integrated Pest Management (IPM) is a fascinating and quickly evolving school of thought when it comes to dealing with pest control. To find out more, get started with the Environmental Protection Agency's introduction to IPM (https://www. epa.gov/managing-pests-schools/introduction-integrated-pest-management) as well as the University of California's statewide IPM program (http://ipm. ucanr.edu/). What are some of the potential benefits of IPM? Are there potential drawbacks, as well?*

▲ Animal control officers routinely trap pests, transport them, and release them away from people.

Butcher/Various Meat-Processing Occupations

Put food on the table-for yourself and others!
Learn a trade you can apply anywhere.
Practice one of the oldest human skills.

WORDS TO UNDERSTAND

dress: here, to dress an animal means to remove its internal organs and scales/fur and prepare it for sale.

fabricated: here, refers to meats such as hot dogs, which are created from raw animal matter.

manual dexterity: the ability to use your hands and fingers with speed and skill.

If you have ever grilled a steak or enjoyed some fried chicken, you have seen the handiwork of a butcher. Butchers take an animal, such as a steer, and kill it, skin it, drain its blood, disembowel it, and cut it into the recognizable cuts of meat that you see in your local stores. The work of a butcher is not for everyone, but there are many related jobs in meat processing, such as slaughterers, meat packers, and fish and poultry cutter. There are workers in processing plants engaged in all steps of the process from live animal to shrink-wrapped package.

◀ Working in a small butcher shop is a great way to learn the skills you can apply anywhe

Is This Job Right for You?

To find out if being a butcher is a good fit for you, read each of the following questions and answer "Yes" or "No."

Yes	*No*	**1.**	*Can you tolerate an animal-processing environment?*
Yes	*No*	**2.**	*Are you comfortable killing animals for food?*
Yes	*No*	**3.**	*Do you have good eye–hand coordination?*
Yes	*No*	**4.**	*Can you learn to wield knives and other cutting implements skillfully and safely?*
Yes	*No*	**5.**	*Can you tolerate getting your clothes sloppy on a daily basis?*
Yes	*No*	**6.**	*Can you work all day on your feet and do some heavy lifting?*
Yes	*No*	**7.**	*Do you understand that meat-processing workers are more prone to injuries than most other workers?*
Yes	*No*	**8.**	*Can you work in the cold environment of a refrigerated room?*
Yes	*No*	**9.**	*Can you serve customers politely?*
Yes	*No*	**10.**	*Can you accurately weigh and label product for sale?*

If you can answer "Yes" to most of these questions, read on to find out more about a career in the meat, poultry, and fish processing industries.

What's the Work Like?

Your work as a meat processor will depend on several factors. The first is the type of animal being cut up. Plants usually specialize in one type of animal, so if you work in a seafood processing plant you will disembowel, descale, and cut up fish, usually removing the head and fins. Some fish are further processed into steaks and fillets, and some are ground into fishmeal. Fish processing is often less removed from sales than other types of meat manufacturing so, as a fish cutter

TALKING MONEY

Employees of the meat processing industry command wages that vary by skill, geographic region, and type of employer. Meat, poultry, and fish cutters in animal slaughtering and processing plants had a median annual salary of $27,040 as of May 2016. Butchers and grocery store meat cutters earned an average salary of $29,870 in the same year. Some meat processing workers are unionized and receive benefits.

▲ Production lines are common in meat processing plants. Here, fish move down a conveyor belt to workers for cutting.

and trimmer (also called fish cleaner), you may **dress** fish as well as sell it directly to whole-sale or retail customers.

Poultry cutters and trimmers work in an environment that is increasingly automated. Workers are usually stationed along a production line where they perform the same routine cutting task on each chicken or turkey that passes along the conveyor. Repetitive stress injuries are common in poultry processing facilities.

Cattle, pigs, sheep, and goats are usually cut into large wholesale slabs of meat at the slaughterhouses where they are killed. At a slaughterhouse, you might be involved in unloading animals destined for slaughter into holding pens, herding them into chutes for stunning and killing them, and then processing the carcass in various ways. Usually the head, limbs, tail, and organs are removed, and the animal is skinned and drained of blood before being cut up. The degree of further processing will depend upon the facility and its customers. Some plants produce cuts such as rounds, ribs, loins, and chunks. Others grind meat into hamburger and manufacture **fabricated** meat products, such as luncheon meats and sausages.

▲ Before it hits supermarket refrigerators, slaughterhouse workers must kill, skin, drain, and cut all types of meat. The large slabs then get trimmed down to the parts you see in the market.

The work of a butcher in a retail or wholesale establishment is different in that the butcher usually works with wholesale cuts of meat to precisely cut and trim them into steaks, chops, roasts, and boneless cuts, and to fulfill specific customer requests.

Who's Hiring?

- Meat, poultry, or fish processing plants

- Wholesalers

- Retail grocery stores

- Butcher shops

- Fish dealers

- Institutional food service facilities

- Slaughterhouses

Where Are the Jobs?

Employees of a meat, poultry, or fish processing plant work in a factory-like atmosphere that is usually white and institutional-looking. The rooms are kept refrigerated to prevent the meat from spoiling, which may take some getting used to for new employees. Floors in slaughterhouses are usually slick with entrails, blood, and other bodily fluids, and the floors of refrigerated processing rooms are damp from condensation, blood, and fat. These conditions, combined with cold temperatures and long hours of standing, lead to considerable risk of slip-and-fall accidents.

The presence and use of many cutting tools, including knives, cleavers, slicers, and power tools result in numerous cutting injuries to workers, including amputations. Although safety measures have been improved, workers in this industry still face considerable risk of serious and disabling injuries.

Butchers and fish cleaners in retail establishments often work in close spaces behind a sales counter. There is usually a refrigerated room for meat storage, and a variety of cutting and wrapping tools, but retail meat processing workers have a less repetitive job than plant workers.

A Typical Day

Here are the highlights for a typical day for a poultry cutter in a poultry processing plant.

Punch in for shift and don hygienic clothing. Most meat processing workers are required to wear hairnets, gloves, and some type of protective covering for their clothing and shoes.

Take up position on production line. You will usually be assigned to a specific spot and task on the production line, performing the same cutting activity, such as clipping off the wings, on each bird that comes along a conveyor system.

▲ One task at a meat processing facility may be to package the sausage links.

NOTES FROM THE FIELD

Butcher, Waltham, Massachusetts

Q: *Where do you work?*

A: I work as a butcher in a family business in Guilford, Connecticut (Guilford Food Center). It is a small grocery store that specializes in fresh meats, deli, bakery, and produce.

Q: *What do you like best about your job?*

A: Being part of a family business allows me to interact with the same clientele on a daily basis and build relationships while providing a community with fresh foods.

Q: *What is the most challenging part of your job?*

A: Coldness in the coolers and freezers. You definitely have to dress for the job, especially in the winter.

Q: *What are the keys to success to being a butcher?*

A: Being honest with your customers and always keeping the product fresh. Customers are smart and will be able to tell if it's not fresh, so to keep them coming back you have to make them happy every single day.

Punch out after shift and go home. When the whistle blows at the end of your shift, you'll punch out on the time clock and you will most likely head home, exhausted, for a much-needed shower and rest.

Start Preparing Now

- Look for an after-school or summer job apprenticing with a local butcher, working the deli or meat counter at one of your neighborhood grocery stores, or, if you live near the coast, cleaning fish.

- Take a cooking class that teaches safe knife handling and use.

- Read up on the Web or at your local library about foodborne illnesses and health and safety regulations.

Training and How to Get It

There are no educational or training qualifications for most meat processing jobs. Most jobs in this field are considered to be very low-skilled occupations, and all the training that you need can be acquired on the job. The exception is the dying profession of butcher. Butchers are skilled in cutting meat to order and preparing specialized ready-to-cook meat products. They perform a greater variety of work than meat processing plant employees. In order to develop these skills, you need to apprentice with a butcher; however, as more meat processing is shifted from the retail sector to manufacturing facilities, the profession of butcher is becoming more of a craft than an everyday trade. Opportunities may be limited compared with the past, but positions may still be found with gourmet vendors.

Health certification is required by some states for certain supervisory roles, but it is usually not relevant to entry-level positions. **Manual dexterity** and good eye–hand coordination are useful for working quickly with cutting tools; some sports and hobbies, such as fishing, may help in developing these skills.

 See what it's like to work at a butcher shop.

Learn the Lingo

Here are a few terms of the trade:

- **Wholesale cut** Portions of a quarter—such as round, loin, rib, chuck, flank, and brisket—that are sold to supermarkets where a butcher chops them into retail cuts.

- **Case-ready** Meat that is prepackaged at a processing plant so it can go directly into the display case in a grocery store.

- **Canner** Lowest USDA grade designation for beef; below cutter, standard, good, select, choice, and prime. Normally used in canned and ground meats and sausages.

Finding a Job

Jobs in the meat processing industry are usually advertised locally. State employment agencies are one place to check for notices of vacancies, as is the classified section of your local newspaper. If you live in a geographic area with many Hispanic immigrants, you might try looking in Spanish-language publications as well. Also, there is no harm in visiting local butcher shops and fish dealers, or the meat section of your local grocery stores, and asking if they are hiring. Since quick, precise, and safe use of various cutting tools is the main component of the job, employers will look for manual dexterity and good eye–hand coordination in potential employees. It will also help if you present a tidy appearance to potential employers, with your nails short and clean and your hair combed or tied back neatly.

Tips for Success

- Have a strong stomach. There's just no other way to put it. Dealing with death, blood, gore, and their associated smells every day is not for everyone.

- Always be mindful of what you are doing—your safety and other people's health depend on it.

▲ **Various processing facilities, including fish processing, can have a very strong odor. Make sure your nose and stomach can handle it!**

Reality Check

The work can be hazardous and isn't always pretty. But you can draw satisfaction from knowing you are providing food for people to put on the table. Your pay may not be great, and some people may find what you do gory, but more than nine in ten North Americans regularly eat meat.

Related Jobs to Consider

Food preparation worker. Food preparation workers assist chefs and cooks in restaurants, grocery stores, and caterers to prepare a large variety of foods to sell to the general public.

LEARN MORE ONLINE

NORTH AMERICAN MEAT INSTITUTE
A trade association for butchers and related meat processing occupations, NAMI publishes an annual meat buyers' guide for butchers, a well-known reference for slicing and grading various cuts of meat. https://www.meatinstitute.org/

AMERICAN ASSOCIATION OF MEAT PROCESSORS
This organization primarily represents employers, not employees, but its site has a lot of information about regulations and food safety. http://www.aamp.com

Baker. Employees of commercial bakeries prepare baked goods for sale. Shift work is common, and some bakers work overnight so that the baked goods are fresh for purchase in the morning.

Fisher. Fishers work on boats to catch various types of seafood for human consumption. Some of the issues with cold and stress and smells are similar to those in the meat processing industry.

How to Move Up

- Advancement in the meat processing industry is usually based on experience. Those employed as butchers usually train under an experienced butcher for a year or two to learn skills involved in preparing specific cuts of meat, tying roasts, and making sausage and other specialized meat products. In some states, health certificates are required to prove that supervisory employees have had training in the safe handling of food to reduce the risk of contamination with foodborne pathogens.

- Employees of meat, poultry, and fish processing plants can move up to team leader and supervisory roles with sufficient experience and communication skills.

TEXT-DEPENDENT QUESTIONS

1. *What are the kinds of meat that butchers and meat processors might work with?*

2. *How do you get trained in this field?*

3. *How might you go about looking for a job?*

4. *What are some alternative careers you might consider?*

RESEARCH PROJECTS

1. *The field of meat processing has a fascinating history, and if you think butchery sounds gory now, it's nothing compared to what the field used to be like. Find out about how far health and safety has come by reading* The Jungle, *a book by Upton Sinclair.*

2. *Large meat processing plants are plentiful, but small, independent butcher shops are getting harder to find. Look on the Internet for independent butchers in your area, and go introduce yourself. Find out what their day-to-day lives are like, including what they like and dislike about their jobs.*

Groundskeeper (Landscaper, Tree Trimmer)

Beautify your community. Work outdoors.
Have variety in your job.

WORDS TO UNDERSTAND

cherry picker: a type of crane with a raised platform.
dehydration: the lack of water in the body.
GED: a substitute for a high school diploma; stands for either general equivalency diploma or general equivalency development.
horticulture: plant care and garden management.

If you like working outside with your hands and enjoy planting flowers and trees, you might want to consider a career as a groundskeeper. Groundskeepers maintain outdoor areas, such as those around public buildings, schools, offices, and residences, as well as parks, golf courses, cemeteries, and athletic fields. The work varies by climate and by season, and it involves much more than just using your hands to dig in the dirt and plant flowers. Groundskeepers also use equipment to mow lawns and prune trees and shrubs, and they sometimes paint and clear snow. If you think you might have a talent for landscape design, starting out as a groundskeeper

◄ Groundskeepers, including landscapers and tree trimmers, are the artists behind the beautifully kept grounds at golf courses, sports arenas, and your home.

a good way to explore your interest and aptitude. There are almost 1.3 million people working as groundskeepers or in related jobs; many of them are Spanish-speaking immigrants. Demand for various types of landscape workers is increasing—you could say it is a growing field.

Is This Job Right for You?

To find out if being a groundskeeper is a good fit for you, read each of the following questions and answer "Yes" or "No."

Yes	*No*	**1.**	*Do you like to work outdoors?*
Yes	*No*	**2.**	*Are you strong and physically fit?*
Yes	*No*	**3.**	*Are you or could you be comfortable using chainsaws, hedge trimmers, mowers, and other potentially dangerous equipment?*
Yes	*No*	**4.**	*Do you like to garden and care for trees, plants, and flowers?*
Yes	*No*	**5.**	*Do you work well on a small team?*
Yes	*No*	**6.**	*Do you speak Spanish, or are you willing to learn?*
Yes	*No*	**7.**	*Do you have the stamina to do physical labor all day?*
Yes	*No*	**8.**	*If you have seasonal allergies, would you be able to manage them?*
Yes	*No*	**9.**	*Can you work independently with directions?*
Yes	*No*	**10.**	*Do you like your work to change with the seasons?*

If you can answer "Yes" to most or all of these questions, read on to find out more about a career as a groundskeeper.

What's the Work Like?

The duties of groundskeepers and landscapers frequently overlap, so sometimes the titles are used interchangeably. Landscapers are responsible for lawn care and maintaining flowers, trees, and other flora on a property. They plant, weed, fertilize, mow, prune, treat for pests and diseases, and generally keep green

TALKING MONEY

Groundskeepers usually earn around $13 per hour. Experienced managers top out at around $21 an hour. The average annual salary of a groundskeeper is around $26,800, although much depends upon experience, location, and the type of grounds being maintained (e.g., an elementary school versus a private estate). Tree trimmers make an average of $16 to $17 per hour.

areas looking tidy and attractive. Groundskeepers are sometimes also responsible for maintaining and painting the exteriors of buildings, putting up and repairing fences, cleaning, deicing and shoveling paved surfaces, and maintaining athletic fields, including pools and courts. Groundskeepers look after outdoor furniture, playground equipment, and other seasonal features. They pick up litter and keep their grounds neat and orderly. They usually repair and maintain all of their equipment.

Tree trimmers prune trees and shrubs using a variety of saws and clippers. Sometimes the trimming is done to keep trees and shrubs healthy or in a shape that is pleasing to the eye. Sometimes trimming is necessary to keep roadways, sidewalks, power lines, and other corridors clear from branches and overgrowth.

▲ Tree trimmers can work down low or up high, making sure that tree growth is healthy and their limbs don't endanger people or property.

Who's Hiring?

- Landscaping companies

- Federal, state, and local governments

- Botanical gardens

- Cemeteries

- Golf courses

- Parks and recreation departments

- Private landscape architects, designers, and contractors

- Private schools, clubs, estates, and residences

- Commercial and residential building complexes

- Colleges and universities

- Athletic complexes

- Amusement parks

Where Are the Jobs?

Your work environment will depend on your geographic climate and the type of employer that you choose. If you work in a cemetery or memorial garden, you may dig graves, mow around graves, and pull weeds to keep the areas around gravestones tidy. If you work for a landscaping company, you will be sent out as a member of a work crew to work on their clients' properties. The clients could be commercial, such as an office complex

TALKING TRENDS

Employment prospects for groundskeepers are good, and the number of jobs is expected to keep pace with other careers through 2024. Governments, private office complexes, and homeowners are increasingly turning to professional landscapers to maintain their properties. Low starting wages and high turnover also create continual job openings in this growing field.

▲ As a groundskeeper, your work environment can vary. This groundskeeper works at a tennis club, tending to the courts. He ensures that the paint lines stay visible and clear of dirt or debris.

with green spaces to mow, trees and shrubs to trim, and flowers to plant and flowerbeds to weed. The work site also could be a private residence, where you will be doing the yard work for a busy family or maybe for an elderly person who needs assistance with lawn care. If you work for the government, you could be mowing highway medians, or planting flowers to beautify roadways, or you could be perched high in a **cherry picker**, trimming branches to keep utility lines clear.

Your schedule will change seasonally. Typically, planting occurs in the spring, followed by fertilizing and weeding through the summer. In the autumn, you might plant bulbs and mulch flowerbeds for the winter. In the winter, you may deice sidewalks and driveways and keep parking lots plowed. If you live in a warm climate, you may be pruning and planting all year round. Some places like to change the plants they have seasonally, so you may be removing flowers and planting new ones in different colors or patterns.

▲ A groundskeeper's job may require snow removal.

Sometimes, too much or too little rain will affect your work schedule. You may have to wait for better weather to do some tasks, or your clients may need you to go around and water to keep the plants alive during dry periods.

A Typical Day

Here are the highlights of a typical day for a groundskeeper at a landscaping company with multiple properties that it is contracted to maintain.

Get your assignment for the day. Find out from your boss what property or properties you will be working on that day and meet up with the rest of your crew.

See what a groundskeeper's typical day looks like.

NOTES FROM THE FIELD

Grounds manager, Palm Beach, Florida

Q: *How did you get your job?*

A: I had been working for nearly four years in a similar type of job (lawn care), and I was made aware of an opening at the Episcopal Church by some parishioners. I wanted to continue working outside (not a desk job), so I went for an interview, and was subsequently hired.

Q: *What do you like best about your job?*

A: I am a "self-starter," and I enjoy working on my own and being my own boss (other than conferring with a grounds committee at the church, I'm on my own). I like the fact that as I prune (cut back), or plant new flora, I see the results of my labors immediately. Due to the high profile nature of our Palm Beach church, the fruits of these labors are seen daily by locals and tourists. I have been able to win awards for the gardens, and it is quite nice to receive those accolades.

Q: *What's the most challenging part of your job?*

A: What challenges you most in the South Florida area is that you are at the mercy of the weather conditions. First, it is hard to find people willing to work in the heat here, as well as someone willing to put in the hours of preparation for hurricane season. Not to mention the time spent with clean up afterwards.

Q: *What are the keys to success to being a groundskeeper?*

A: Weather conditions can make you or break you . . . and when they are optimal, it allows for flora and fauna to have a good growing season and therefore creates quite a showplace for parishioners and tourists to walk through and enjoy. It is imperative to keep learning about your craft, because knowing your climate, terrain, and plant materials, and how they adapt to the environment here, is crucial, especially when your work is in the public eye on a daily basis.

Prepare your equipment. Make sure that all of the tools and safety equipment that you will need for the day's tasks are loaded onto your crew's vehicles. If you will be planting, check that you have the right number and type of plants.

Check over your job site before you leave. At the end of each day, or whenever a job is finished, check that the area where you were working is left clean and neat, and that no work tools or trash are left behind.

Start Preparing Now

• Get a summer, weekend, or after-school job with a local landscaping or lawn care company. Most hire high school students, especially in the busy summer months. Working for a landscape company is the perfect way to find out if the job is for you.

• If you do not already speak Spanish, take a Spanish class at your high school. Most landscape workers speak Spanish as their first language, and knowing the language will help you communicate with other members of your work crew.

• Take classes in botany and **horticulture**, if your high school offers them. Look for classes offered by botanical gardens or community education groups. Get books from the library to learn the names and growing conditions for plants local to your area.

• Volunteer at a community garden. Start your own garden plot or even just a window box. If you live in a suburban or rural area, offer to mow lawns and weed for neighbors. Put up signs offering your services at reasonable rates.

Training and How to Get It

Most groundskeepers and landscapers learn on the job. Some knowledge of plants is useful, but it is not a requirement to get most entry-level jobs. Some employers will not insist that you have a high school diploma or **GED**, but it may be a requirement for certain types of certification.

You will need to learn how to handle delicate plants without damaging them, and how to plant them and care for them so that they will grow in their new locations. You will also need to learn how to prune trees and shrubs, weed flowerbeds, and mow lawns. In some climates, you will have to learn to operate plows and snow blowers.

Much of your on-the-job training will involve learning how to use, maintain, and repair the tools of your trade safely. Experienced groundskeepers will teach you how to use equipment like chainsaws, trimmers, mowers, leaf blowers, and wood chippers safely and effectively in your work.

Some jobs will require you to drive your equipment to the job site, so a driver's license and a clean driving record will be essential for these jobs.

There are many certification programs for landscape professionals. Certification can increase your employability and raise your pay. (See "Learn More Online" at the end of this chapter for more information.)

Learn the Lingo

Here are a few words you'll hear as a groundskeeper, landscaper, or tree trimmer:

- **Greenskeeper** The name for a groundskeeper who maintains a golf course. In addition to the typical duties of a groundskeeper, a greenskeeper must move the holes around on the greens to add variety to the course, and make sure that the ball washers, tee markers, canopies, and other equipment specific to a golf course are in good repair.

- **Balled and burlapped** Also "B&B," this term refers to the root ball of a tree or shrub being wrapped in burlap for transport after it has been dug up to be transplanted to a new location.

- **Dethatching** Dethatching is the removal of a dead layer of turf-grass so that new sod can be laid down or other plantings can take place. Landscapers do a lot of dethatching.

Finding a Job

Finding a job as a groundskeeper can be as easy as walking into the closest landscaping company and asking if they are hiring. You can also contact your local parks and recreation department. Sometimes parks, gardens, athletic fields, and other recreational facilities will have signs saying who maintains them. Call them up and tell them you are interested in working for them. You can also contact local golf courses and cemeteries to see if they are hiring entry-level laborers. Most employers will not require that you have experience, but tell them about any landscape work that you have done and convey that you are eager to learn on the job. Enthusiasm and good communication skills will impress a potential employer.

▲ These B&B trees are wrapped and ready for transport.

If you see a local building with good landscaping, ask the owner who does their work for them. If you see a crew out working, ask them who they work for.

Tips for Success

- Take care in your work. Plants that look attractive and healthy will show your boss and your clients that you are careful and that you take pride in your work. On the other hand, unevenly trimmed trees and shrubs, or dirt and branches left around a job site, could eventually cost you your job.

- Learn to estimate how long it takes you to complete tasks, so that you can set realistic goals for yourself and achieve them. Your employers will appreciate this, and your workday will be calmer.

Reality Check

Landscaping work can involve long hours out in the hot sun in the summer and in the cold clearing snow in the winter. Make sure that you dress appropriately for the weather, wear sunscreen, and drink lots of water to avoid **dehydration**. If you are not given training in how to use the equipment you need for a job, ask. It is better to tell your boss that you have never used a chainsaw or wood chipper than to fake it and wind up injured.

Related Jobs to Consider

Pest-management technician. Pest-management technicians apply chemical sprays to control insects and weeds, prevent diseases, and stimulate the growth of decorative plants and crops. You could work for chemical lawn care services, farmers, golf courses, or specialized pest-control companies.

LEARN MORE ONLINE

TREE CARE INDUSTRY ASSOCIATION.
This site contains everything you need to know about becoming a certified arborist. You can look up tree care companies by zip code and get information on careers in arboriculture. http://www.tcia.org/

PROFESSIONAL LANDCARE NETWORK (PLANET).
PLANET provides information for both commercial and residential lawn care professionals. It offers certification exams for various categories of landscape technicians. http://www.landcarenetwork.org

PROFESSIONAL GROUNDS MANAGEMENT SOCIETY (PGMS)
PGMS is a resource for institutional grounds managers, such as groundskeepers for colleges and universities, parks and recreation facilities, commercial and residential complexes, cemeteries, and municipalities. They provide education for professional development and certification. http://www.pgms.org

Forestry worker or logger. There are a variety of jobs related to forestry that you might consider. Foresters can be involved in conservation and management of forests—or they can work for logging companies, cutting down and hauling trees.

Agricultural worker. Agricultural workers perform a variety of tasks on farms and ranches, from planting and fertilizing crops to picking and packaging produce. Agricultural workers may also work with animals in the meat and dairy industries.

Nursery employee. Employees of a commercial nursery grow plants that will be purchased and transplanted. They care for seedlings and advise customers on which plants to choose for their growing environment.

How to Move Up

- Become a supervisor. You can move up to a supervisory role in your job with experience and good organizational and communication skills.

- Become a landscape contractor by starting your own business. After you have been a supervisor for a while, you may want to strike out on your own and start your own landscape business. You will need good references to build up a client base, and have the ability to hire and train your own employees. Some states have licensing requirements for landscape contractors, so check the laws in your state.

- Become a landscape designer or landscape architect. If you have an interest and a talent for creating attractive landscape design plans, you may be able to get hired by clients just to do design work. It takes a four-year degree to become a certified landscape architect, but you can usually work your way through school.

- Become an arborist. You will need to learn about proper tree care and how to choose the right type of tree for different environments. You will supervise tree trimmers and planters.

TEXT-DEPENDENT QUESTIONS

1. *What's the difference between a landscaper and a groundskeeper?*

2. *How might you go about getting work in this field?*

3. *What does a greenskeeper do?*

4. *What are some ways you might move up in this field?*

RESEARCH PROJECTS

1. *Start learning about groundskeeping by improving the space where you live. If you live in an apartment building or near a park, there is probably already a grounds crew working there; introduce yourself and ask about what they do. If you live in a house, the "grounds crew" may be your parents, who will be delighted to have some help. You can easily turn this into a weekend business by offering your services around the neighborhood.*

2. *If there's no one around who can teach you about landscaping, there are lots of do-it-yourself books (check the home-improvement section of your bookstore or ask your librarian for suggestions) and Web sites. Get started at DIY Landscaping (http://www.diynetwork.com/how-to/outdoors/landscaping) or DIY Landscaping Projects for Beginners (https://www.thespruce.com/diy-landscaping-projects-4119886).*

▲ Noise-reduction protective ear muffs are an important piece of safety equipment when working with loud equipment.

Forestry/Conservation/Logging-Crew Member

Work outdoors all year round. Help prevent forest fires. Join a traditional industry.

One of the most important natural resources in the United States is our forests. Our nation's forests serve many functions, providing a source of natural beauty and recreation for humans, a carbon sink to cleanse the air we breathe, a habitat for wildlife, and a source of wood and other forest products. The forestry sector provides a variety of job opportunities for workers with a high school diploma. In 2014, there were about 53,000 loggers, 14,000 forest conservation workers, and about 40,000 professional tree trimmers. Most of the work does not require education beyond the high school level as it consists mainly of operating heavy equipment, such as feller-bunchers and loaders, that you can really only learn to do on the job, not in a classroom. Logging requires a great deal of physical strength and **stamina**, as well as the ability to operate complicated heavy machinery with strict attention to safety.

◀ Cutting down trees can be a very dangerous job. Here, logging-crew members use chainsaws to remove limbs at the top of a tree.

Is This Job Right for You?

To find out if being a logger is a good fit for you, read each of the following statements and answer "Yes" or "No."

Yes	No	1.	*Are you willing to work outdoors in any weather?*
Yes	No	2.	*Are you willing to do work that is physically demanding and hazardous?*
Yes	No	3.	*Are you willing to work in isolated areas?*
Yes	No	4.	*Are you comfortable operating heavy machinery, or at least willing to give it a try?*
Yes	No	5.	*Are you healthy, strong, and physically fit?*
Yes	No	6.	*Do you have a lot of stamina?*
Yes	No	7.	*Can you exercise good judgment?*
Yes	No	8.	*Are you mechanically inclined, and could you learn to maintain heavy equipment?*
Yes	No	9.	*Are you willing to commute a long distance to a job site?*
Yes	No	10.	*Are you willing to do a job that requires hard, physical labor every day?*

If you can answer "Yes" to most of these questions, read on to find out more about a career in forestry.

What's the Work Like?

There are many kinds of jobs in this field. Many loggers work as tree fallers, using chainsaws and falling machines to cut down trees in a forest and transport the logs to saw mills. But the work of a logging crew is divided into many specific jobs. Choke setters fasten steel cables and chains onto felled trees so that they can be skidded to trucks and waterways for transport. Other logging equipment operators load and unload logs at railways and sawmills. There are

TALKING MONEY

Average hourly pay for loggers in 2016 was $18.07, for tree trimmers it was $17.94, and for forest and conservation workers it was $12.95. Larger firms usually paid higher wages, as did companies in Alaska and the Pacific Northwest. Loggers get few benefits, such as health insurance, and smaller firms might not even provide safety equipment. Government workers tend to get better benefits than those in the private sector.

▲ Tree fallers use chainsaws to make a series of cuts at the base of the tree.

also rigging slingers, chasers, log sorters, markers, movers, and chippers, each with their own machinery and tasks. On a typical logging crew of four to eight members, you would be expected to learn to do several of these jobs well, including maintaining the equipment that you use.

Once the trees get to a sawmill, graders and scalers take over—using saws, and cutting and planning devices—to prepare the logs to be sold for various consumer and industrial uses. Today, there are very few sawmills operating in the United States. Most felled trees are shipped abroad to be processed because of cheaper labor; then the wood may come back to the United States to be used in construction or the paper industry or for furniture.

As a forest conservation worker, you might thin woodlands to prevent forest fires in dry areas. You also would plant seedlings to regenerate deforested areas and **abate** infestations of insects that damage trees. Sorting and preparing seedlings for transplanting might be part of your duties. Controlling soil erosion is another job you would have as a forest conservation worker. Soil erosion is a problem in areas that have been deforested because tree roots help hold the soil in place. Once the trees are gone, soil can wash into nearby waterways and cause problems for fish and for people who live downstream.

If you work for the government on public lands, you would also clean campsites, possibly including rest rooms and recreational facilities. You would have to clear debris from roadways around the campground and keep trails clear of encroaching underbrush. Cataloging data about forests might form part of your duties. You might take a handheld device into the woods to note the types, ages, and health of various trees and other species of flora and fauna around them. These data might be used to track endangered species, maintain forest health and species diversity, or provide information to potential buyers about what types and sizes of trees are available for logging.

It's also possible that you could work on a tree farm. Would you like to grow Christmas trees? There are also tree farms that specialize in ornamental trees or trees for specific uses, like furniture. On a tree farm, you'd be responsible for planting seedlings, controlling weeds and other pests, pruning the trees to encourage them to grow in a certain shape, and harvesting and wrapping them for shipping. In some places, you might tap trees for syrup, or harvest mosses, pine cones, and other plant life that are found around trees. About 30 percent of forestry workers are self-employed as independent contractors.

 Learn more about being a forest conservation worker.

Who's Hiring?

- USDA Forest Service

- Logging contractors

- Sawmills and planing mills

- Self

- Tree farms

- State and local government

Where Are the Jobs?

You'll spend most of your time working outdoors, unless you happen to work in a sawmill or planing mill. In the north, most logging is done in the winter because the frozen ground makes it easier to move the logs. Logging can also be done in very dry weather, but rain and mud can cause delays to the extent that you may have to find other work during the off-season. Loggers frequently have to travel a long way to get to their job sites, and some even stay in bunkhouses. But it depends upon the area in which you live, so don't let that discourage you from looking.

TALKING TRENDS

Job opportunities in the forestry sector are projected to grow slower than average for the next decade. Openings in the logging industry will result mostly from attrition—the job attracts young men who often move on to less hazardous jobs as they age. Government forestry jobs concerned with preventing wildfires may grow slightly, but the increasing mechanization of the timber harvesting industry, along with cheaper foreign labor, is likely to result in more layoffs than jobs in the private sector for the foreseeable future.

A Typical Day

Here are the highlights for a typical day for a forest conservation worker working for a private timber company, although most of these tasks would be the same if you were working for the government.

Trim or cut down diseased trees. Using hand tools like chainsaws, cut down trees that have been marked as diseased or otherwise undesirable and remove them from the site.

Spray trees with pesticides. If insects or fungi are attacking the trees, you may be asked to spray them with insecticides and fungicides. You might also spray herbicides on the undergrowth to ensure that other vegetation there does not compete with the trees for light and nutrients in the soil. Make sure that you wear protective equipment, which may include a breathing mask, even if your employer does not require it or provide it.

Perform duties assigned by a professional forester. These may include examining trees and doing such tasks as measuring them, marking them, and counting them. You might be asked to conduct controlled burns of underbrush or boundary areas, or to mark boundary lines with paint.

▲ After trees are cut down, the logs are transported to a sawmill or planing mill. The logs are processed by machines and then cut to different sizes. This is where your two-by-fours are cut.

Start Preparing Now

Look up information on forestry-related careers and conservation on the Internet or at your local library. There is a lot of research you can do now to help narrow down the area where you might like to work.

- The USDA Forest Service has a site that collects job and internship opportunities with the agency: https://www.fs.fed.us/working-with-us/opportunities-for-young-people

- A summer job in a nursery now can help you land a forestry-related job later. And many nurseries are happy to hire high school students to perform manual labor in the busy spring and summer seasons. Ask around at your local nurseries.

- Christmas tree sellers often hire high school kids to help sell trees between Thanksgiving and Christmas.

Training and How to Get It

As stated earlier, most of your training will be on the job, learning to operate expensive equipment that is used just for the logging industry. When you start out as a logging-crew member, you will be given less-skilled work, such as clearing brush.

Some vocational and technical schools offer two-year degree courses in fields such as conservation and forest harvesting. There are also training programs in most states that lead to logger certification. A degree or certificate that includes both classroom study and fieldwork might give you an edge in a shrinking job market.

Learn the Lingo

Here are a few terms of the trade:

- **Dibble bars and hoedads** These are the funny names for digging and planting tools that are used to plant tree seedlings.

- **Buckers** *Buck* means cut, and buckers are members of a logging crew who use chain saws to trim off tree tops and branches and cut logs into shorter lengths.

- **Chokers** Chokers are steel cables or chains that are attached to felled trees in order to skid (drag) them to the roadway so that they can be sorted and put on trucks.

Finding a Job

In order to find a job as a logger, you should look online for leads on job openings in your area. There are many state and regional logging trade associations, and they usually list local job openings on their Web sites. The Associated Oregon Loggers is the largest in the country (http://www.oregonloggers.org), but, if you live in another area with an active forest resources industry, a quick search should find an association near you. Many logging contractors are independent businessmen with small crews that they hire seasonally for logging jobs. For these employers, you may be expected to provide your own safety equipment and have some experience using chainsaws and other equipment. The way to find out is to ask local contractors if they are willing to take you on and train you. The same goes for sawmills and planing mills. If there is one where you live, walk in and ask the foreman if he is hiring. It never hurts to introduce yourself and ask if there are any jobs available.

About half of all forestry workers are employed by the government so checking local, state, or federal government Web sites for job listings is a good place to start, especially if you are interested in conservation rather than timber processing.

Tips for Success

• Be safety conscious. Remember, logging is among the most hazardous jobs in the United States. Make sure that you wear a hardhat, eye protection, and—especially important—ear protection, as the noise from the machinery and the falling trees can damage your

▲ Loggers operate heavy equipment and machinery, which can be dangerous.

hearing over time. You will also need to wear tough boots. If you are doing a controlled burn, you will have to be super careful about containing the fire and not getting burned or inhaling smoke. Finally, you will need to follow all necessary safety precautions when handling pesticides.

- Earn the trust and respect of your colleagues through hard work and honest dealing.

Reality Check

According to the U.S. Bureau for Labor Statistics, logging is the most dangerous job in the United States. It ranked number one in the annual statistics of deaths on the job, with 132 deaths per 100,000 workers from 2014 to 2015—more than twice the rate of the next-most dangerous job of fisherman. Think seriously about the risks involved in this line of work before you decide that logging is the career for you.

Related Jobs to Consider

Grounds maintenance worker. These laborers look after the landscaping in a variety of settings. The work is not highly skilled, or highly paid, but it varies seasonally and you could work at college campuses, golf courses, sports facilities, corporate office complexes, malls, schools, parks, private homes, and anyplace else with landscaping that must be trimmed, planted, watered, and otherwise maintained.

Material moving operators. These workers use heavy equipment to move earth, debris, construction materials, and whatever else weighs too much to lift by hand. This job involves operating large machinery, and the work can vary seasonally. Demand for these workers is high, and you can train on the job. Pay is higher for those workers who learn to operate specialized equipment, such as cranes and pumps.

Forest ranger or firefighter. Forest rangers patrol forests to make sure that people using the forests for recreation are safe and following all rules about campfires, trash disposal, vehicle use, etc. Firefighters put out forest fires and try to prevent fires from spreading to developed areas.

LEARN MORE ONLINE

SOCIETY OF AMERICAN FORESTERS
This site contains lots of information about careers in forestry, including a special section just for students. https://www.eforester.org/

FOREST RESOURCES ASSOCIATION, INC.
This organization provides information about the forest products industry and lists programs that offer training for logging-related occupations. http://forestresources.org

USDA FOREST SERVICE
Federal government Web site contains detailed maps and information about national forests by state and name, as well as job listings. http://www.fs.fed.us

How to Move Up

- As you gain experience and prove your reliability and skill, you are likely to be given increased responsibilities. If you ask to learn how to use more sophisticated and specialized equipment, you may become able to supervise other loggers and train new ones. You might specialize in one phase of timber processing, and spend most of your time operating the equipment for that task. You might even decide to work for a company, such as John Deere, that makes logging equipment, and go around demonstrating it and training workers in how to use it.

- In the area of conservation, you could go to school and get a four-year degree in conservation biology or forestry. A degree would open up a whole new range of forestry jobs for you, at higher pay and with benefits.

TEXT-DEPENDENT QUESTIONS

1. *What are some of the specific jobs on a logging crew?*

2. *What tasks do forest conservation workers perform?*

3. *How might you start looking for a job?*

4. *What are some related careers you could consider instead?*

RESEARCH PROJECTS

1. *There are several reality shows that focus on loggers, but it's important to keep in mind that TV shows are inclined to show only the most dramatic aspects of a situation. For a more well-rounded understanding of what logging is about, try books like* Deadfall *by James LeMonds,* Lumberjack *by William S. Crow, and* Tall Trees, Tough Men *by Robert E. Pike. Also seek out this interview with a logger named Chuck Carlson ("The Life of a Lumberjack," https://www.theatlantic.com/business/archive/2016/11/logger/507848/).*

2. *The philosophies and practices that guide forest conservation are complicated and have changed a lot over time. Find out more about the thinking behind forest conservation practices by spending some time on the Web sites of the Center for International Forestry Research (http://www.cifor.org) and the World Agroforestry Centre (http://www.worldagroforestry.org/).*

Nursery/Greenhouse Assistant

Turn your green thumb into a livelihood. Make living plants your living. Nurture the next generation of vegetation.

WORDS TO UNDERSTAND

hydroponically: grown in nutrient-rich water instead of soil.

irrigation: a mechanical process that brings water to plants.

transplant: here, moving a plant from one place or container to another.

When you are outside, look around and you are likely to see grass, trees, shrubs, and flowers. They may be in the yards of homeowners, or in the landscaping borders that add a bit of cheerful nature to schools, office buildings, apartment complexes, hospitals, and other developments. These plants do not usually go into the ground as seeds. More often, seedlings are grown in commercial nurseries and greenhouses, and, when they have reached a certain size, the plants are purchased and transplanted into their new homes. Nursery and greenhouse assistants are the people who grow these plants from seeds, and then sell them to individuals and businesses.

◀ Nursery and greenhouse assistants make sure that plants, fruits, and vegetables are healthy, attractive, and readily available for sellers.

Is This Job Right for You?

To find out if being a nursery/greenhouse assistant is a good fit for you, read each of the following statements and answer "Yes" or "No."

Yes	No	1. *Have you been told that you have a "green thumb," and do you enjoy growing things?*
Yes	No	2. *Are you okay with getting wet and dirty on a job?*
Yes	No	3. *Are you willing to do physical labor all day at your workplace?*
Yes	No	4. *Can you tolerate working with pesticides, herbicides, and fungicides?*
Yes	No	5. *Can you see yourself digging in dirt all day long?*
Yes	No	6. *Are you okay with being on your feet all day, and doing some heavy lifting?*
Yes	No	7. *Would you enjoy helping customers choose plants that are appropriate for their homes and businesses?*
Yes	No	8. *Would you like to learn how to take care of many different types of plants?*
Yes	No	9. *Can you carefully handle delicate plants, such as seedlings?*
Yes	No	10. *Do you like the idea of helping things grow?*

If you can answer "Yes" to most of these questions, read on to find out more about a career in the nursery business.

What's the Work Like?

Nursery and greenhouse workers function as the parents of commercially grown plants. They raise them from seeds and then send them out into the world. You will have the satisfaction of seeing seeds that you planted in tiny flats sprout and grow into sturdy plants that you will then have to

TALKING MONEY

Nursery and greenhouse work is extremely low paying. The average hourly rate in 2016 was $11.45 per hour. That said, the pay scale ranges a great deal depending on the part of the country you're in: for example, in parts of Nevada and North Dakota, the average pay is more than $17 per hour, while in parts of Georgia and Florida, the average hourly pay is less than $10. Nursery and greenhouse workers are rarely unionized. Some jobs come with benefits, including health and retirement savings accounts. Jobs in rural areas tend to come with housing; jobs in urban areas are less likely to offer housing as part of the compensation package.

▲ Some plants and vegetables, like lettuce, can be grown in a greenhouse with the assistance of hydroponics.

transplant into larger containers. Each day, you will water, fertilize, prune, weed, and otherwise tend to your assigned plants. You may care for flowers, vines, shrubs, trees, or other flora. Some nurseries and greenhouses specialize in one type of plant, such as roses. A greenhouse full of roses smells wonderful and looks beautiful. Greenhouses are also used to grow out-of-season fruits and vegetables or to grow them in a climate that would not sustain them outdoors; you might be tending strawberries in a greenhouse in December, watching snow fall outside the warm glass. Occasionally, plants are grown **hydroponically**: These plants require slightly different care, which you would learn on the job.

The work you will do may seem repetitive at times as you may have many rows of identical plants, all in the same stage of growth and all needing the same type of attention. You'll need to exercise great care in handling delicate plants, especially during the transplanting phase when they are most vulnerable.

If you deal directly with customers, you will need to be knowledgeable about what types of plants will grow best in that customer's type of soil and climate. You'll need to ask questions such as how much shade the proposed planting area has and what type of drainage. The more you know about ideal growing conditions for your plants, the more satisfied your customers will be.

Who's Hiring?

- Commercial nurseries

- Commercial greenhouses

- Specialty greenhouses and nurseries, such as rose growers

- Commercial hydroponic greenhouses

- Nursery sections of major retailers

- Small, family-owned nurseries and greenhouses

- University research departments

- Agricultural product packing and shipping companies

TALKING TRENDS

Although agricultural jobs in general are expected to decline for the foreseeable future, nursery and greenhouse job opportunities are likely to increase. This is because the need for landscaping will grow hand-in-hand with new buildings and housing developments. These jobs tend not to be impacted by the market forces that are causing other agricultural jobs to decline. Job turnover is high due to low pay and poor working conditions, making it relatively easy to get a job.

Where Are the Jobs?

Your job environment will depend on many factors, including the type of employer you choose, whether large or small, the climate in your geographic location, and the types of plants grown in the nursery or greenhouse where you are employed. If you tend trees or shrubs, you will probably be working outdoors. If you tend delicate plants in a cold climate, you will be working in a greenhouse that is heated to a temperature much warmer than the outside air.

Your workplace will also vary by size. Huge commercial growers can have multiple, cavernous greenhouses on one site, with hundreds of workers, whereas a mom-and-pop nursery may have only one or two small greenhouses, a few rows of trees and shrubs out back, and a few employees.

The biggest difference in your work environment will depend upon whether you grow food or decorative plants, and whether or not you sell directly to the public. If you grow food, you may have little to do at certain phases of its growth, but then you may have to work long

▲ Temperature and humidity control are extremely important to growing healthy plants indoors.

hours harvesting and packing your produce when it is just ripe. If you sell directly to the public, you may need additional training in plant selection, and you are more likely to work for a business that sells a variety of decorative plants rather than a monoculture enterprise.

Finally, universities and agricultural corporations employ greenhouse assistants in their research departments. These workers tend plants that are grown for experiments on plant genetics, pesticide resistance, and many other purposes. This can be an exciting environment if you are interested in science.

A Typical Day

Here are the highlights for a typical day for a greenhouse assistant working for a large, commercial greenhouse.

Prepare soil for planting. Using gardening tools, mix soil so that it has the appropriate nutrients, density, and acidity for your seeds. Fill each compartment of large planting trays with the soil.

Plant seeds. Place appropriate number of seeds in each compartment in your flats, at the depth needed for that particular seed to sprout.

Water plants and check equipment. Your newly planted seeds will need to be watered right away. Then you will need to check the **irrigation** system in your greenhouse to make sure that it releases the appropriate amount of water or mist, at the correct intervals, for your plants.

 Learn more about hydroponics.

Start Preparing Now

- Get an after-school, weekend, or summer job at a local greenhouse or nursery. Some nurseries hire high school students to help sell Christmas trees, wreaths, and other greenery during the holiday season.

- If your high school offers any plant-related science classes, take them. Look around for classes in your community as well.

- Get a driver's license and maintain a clean driving record. Some jobs will require driving, and potential employers will look at your driving history.

Training and How to Get It

Although you can get a job at a nursery or greenhouse with a high school degree, some technical colleges offer Nursery/Greenhouse Technician certificate programs that may give you an edge in getting a job. These programs will teach you such skills as plant identification, pest control, fertilizer use, irrigation techniques, garden center management, and even greenhouse design, construction, and maintenance. Some sort of certification is usually necessary to move up to a supervisory position. In some cases, your employer may be willing to pay for this training—it never hurts to ask.

To figure out what training is most appropriate for you, consider where you might work. The skills needed to grow dwarf varieties of trees outdoors are somewhat different from those needed to grow red peppers hydroponically indoors. In either case, you will be trained on the job. The most important training you can have prior to finding employment is in how to

NOTES FROM THE FIELD

Greenhouse Assistant, *Biology Department,*
State University of New York, Binghamton, New York

Q: *How did you get your job?*

A: At the entry level positions (retail greenhouse businesses), I was chosen for the job due to having some plant-culture background, primarily through the cooperative extension's Master Gardener Program. As I moved up in the green industry, I was chosen for management positions based on higher education in plant science, internships at a public garden, and holding a license as a Commercial Pesticide Applicator.

Q: *What do you like best about your job?*

A: I like working in an environment that brings great joy to visitors of the collections in the teaching greenhouse. As I moved up the levels, the responsibilities increased, but so did the ability to set my own priorities and workday.

Q: *What's the most challenging part of your job?*

A: Entry-level retail positions come with the challenges of dealing with many different customers; and patience, diplomacy, cheerfulness, and self-assurance are all necessary to get through the day. The hours may be on weekends and holidays, making your own family gatherings come second. Many duties can become routine very rapidly.

Q: *What are the keys to success to being a greenhouse assistant?*

A: The most important key has been to seek continuing education, thus putting me in a position to move from retail jobs to academia, where there is a chance to tailor my work to my personality and goals.

follow directions. Your work will be largely independent, but you will need to follow instructions, especially when you are new to the job and cannot yet judge from experience whether plants need pruning or watering, or if they are ready to be transplanted. It also helps if you are self-motivated as you may be working with little supervision.

Learn the Lingo

Here are a few terms of the trade:

- **Hydroponics** A system of growing plants in nutrient-enriched water instead of soil.

- **pH** pH is a measurement of the concentration of hydrogen ions in soil, fertilizer, or irrigation water. The higher the pH, the more alkaline the solution. A lower pH indicates a more acidic solution. Different plants require different pH levels to thrive. The acidic soil in which a pine tree grows, for example, will kill most other plants.

- **Horticulturist** Someone who works in plant propagation, doing research into plant physiology and biochemistry with the goal of improving crop yields, transportability, and appearance.

▲ **These students work together to tend herbs and edible flowers as a part of a horticulture program.**

Finding a Job

Finding a job as a greenhouse or nursery assistant is relatively easy since most of the training occurs on the job. Employers will usually hire high school graduates, or candidates with a GED (general educational development) credential, without experience. If you have appropriate certification, you will be eligible for a higher-level job, at higher rates of pay, but don't be shy about applying for an entry-level job before you have any credentials. You can gain valuable experience at the same time you are earning certification.

Greenhouse and nursery jobs may be advertised in your local paper, but you can also just walk into local businesses and ask if they are hiring. University jobs will most likely be advertised on the university's Web site. Check for employment listings in the human resources section. You can also make contact with greenhouse managers at local universities directly and ask them to keep you in mind when they have an opening. If they get funding for a research project and find themselves in need of assistants, they may give you a call. Present yourself to potential employers as dependable and willing to follow directions. Show an interest in plants and a willingness and enthusiasm to learn quickly.

Tips for Success

- Keep upgrading your skills. If you are motivated to study plant science at the college level, obtain certification as a nursery technician, or get licensed as a pesticide applicator, you will be able to command a higher wage and move up to management roles.

- Pay close attention to detail—those plants aren't just fragile, they cost money!

Reality Check

Agricultural jobs, including nursery and greenhouse work, are generally low-paying. This is due to the fact that entry-level jobs require few skills. In some areas, agricultural jobs are held mainly by immigrants whose lack of education and inability to speak English prevent them from obtaining higher-paying jobs.

Related Jobs to Consider

Grounds maintenance worker. These laborers look after landscaping in a variety of settings. The work is not highly skilled, or highly paid, but it varies seasonally and you could work at college campuses, golf courses, sports facilities, corporate office complexes, malls, schools, parks, private homes, and anyplace else with landscaping that must be trimmed, planted, watered, and otherwise maintained.

Farmworker/agricultural technician. These laborers plant, nurture, harvest, and pack produce on large commercial farms.

Forest, conservation, or logging worker. This field involves working in managed forests to cut and haul trees for commercial uses. It is also possible to work for government agencies, such as the USDA Forest Service, overseeing the condition of state and national forests.

LEARN MORE ONLINE

AMERICAN HORT
This is a membership organization that provides information on education and research. It follows legal developments related to the professions and lobbies on behalf of its members. http://americanhort.org/

COLORADO NURSERY AND GREENHOUSE ASSOCIATION
Like similar organizations in states throughout the country, this Colorado association offers valuable information about the specifics of the industry in its area. Look for the industry associations in your state. http://www.coloradonga.org

How to Move Up

• As you gain experience and prove your reliability, you may be given increased responsibilities. But you may find your work becoming routine and there may be a limit to how much your duties can change if you do not obtain additional education and training. Find out if your employer will pay all or part of the cost of a one-year certificate program at a technical college or a two-year associate's degree in plant sciences at a community college. Also find out if there is demand in your area for workers with specific licensing, such as pesticide application. Some four-year colleges have programs that will allow you to work full or part time while earning your degree, and your employer may pay for your studies.

TEXT-DEPENDENT QUESTIONS

1. Who hires workers in this field?

2. What are hydroponics?

3. Where can you look for jobs?

4. How might you move up in this field?

RESEARCH PROJECTS

1. The big home-improvement chains all depend on greenhouses to stock their gardening section. Visit a store near you and ask to talk to a staff member in charge of gardening. Find out how the process works: Where do the plants come from? How often are they restocked or switched over as the seasons change? Who decides what plants are offered? Who looks after the plants once they arrive, and what does that process involve?

2. Find out if you like helping things grow by starting some seeds: all you need is some dirt, a few seeds, and a sunny window. If you want to get more sophisticated, ask your school librarian to suggest some gardening books or check the home-improvement section of your bookstore. You can also look for advice on sites like Container Gardening (https://bonnieplants.com/container-gardening) and Basics of Gardening (http://www.basicsofgardening.com/).

Forest Firefighter/ Range Aide

Work for the government—outdoors!
Take a stand on forest health. Fight wildfires.

WORDS TO UNDERSTAND

camaraderie: friendship and mutual trust among a group.

fire hazard: anything that has the potential for starting a fire or making one worse.

municipal: relating to a city or town.

probationary: describes an initial period where a person is observed and evaluated.

wildland: land that is uncultivated by people.

Wilderness takes care of itself. Trees die and decay, and new saplings sprout. Insects, fungi, and bacteria feed on both dead and living tree matter. Lightning strikes cause fires that may burn huge swaths of forest, which then slowly regenerate, with new green seedlings poking up through the charred, dead wood. But life in an orchard, tree farm, or state forest is quite different. A fire is a disaster, which can cause danger to nearby houses or burn down orchard trees that supply someone's livelihood. Likewise, infestations by insects can be economically devastating. These types of managed woodlands require the availability of forest firefighters, also called

◀ Forest firefighters must maintain fires from an assortment of causes. This fire resulted from a lightning strike in the forest.

wildland firefighters, as well as forest fire inspectors and forestry aides to assist professional foresters or tree farmers in maintaining the health of their managed forest or orchard.

Is This Job Right for You?

To find out if being a forest firefighter/range aide is a good fit for you, read each of the following statements and answer "Yes" or "No."

Yes *No*	**1.**	*Are you willing to work outdoors in any weather?*
Yes *No*	**2.**	*Are you willing to do work that is physically demanding and hazardous?*
Yes *No*	**3.**	*Are you willing to work in isolated areas, far from city and town?*
Yes *No*	**4.**	*Are you comfortable operating heavy machinery, or are you willing to give it a try?*
Yes *No*	**5.**	*Are you healthy, strong, and physically fit?*
Yes *No*	**6.**	*Do you have a lot of stamina?*
Yes *No*	**7.**	*Can you exercise good judgment?*
Yes *No*	**8.**	*Do you have a desire to fight fires, and do you fully understand the risks of this job?*
Yes *No*	**9.**	*Are you willing to commute a long distance to your job site?*
Yes *No*	**10.**	*Are you okay with a job that requires hard, physical labor every day?*

If you can answer "Yes" to most of these questions, read on to find out more about a career in the field of forestry.

What's the Work Like?

As a forestry aide, you may work under the supervision of a professional forester, performing such duties as thinning woodlands to prevent forest fires in dry areas. You also would plant seedlings to regenerate deforested areas and abate infestations of insects that dry out trees and make them more susceptible to conflagration. Your work will overlap with that of a

TALKING MONEY

Forest aides earned an average of $12.92 per hour in 2016, while forest fire inspectors earned an average of $21.30 per hour. Meanwhile, the median hourly earnings of firefighters in 2016 was $23.09. Pay rises with seniority, and firefighters are always paid overtime. The job also comes with benefits and a pension.

forest conservation worker, so you might want to look at Chapter 6 for more information on possible duties.

There is a big difference in what work you would perform as a forestry aide in a national or state forest and in an orchard. Trees on a tree farm are grown and maintained as monoculture crops, so the ecosystem resembles that of a field of corn more than a wild forest. Irrigation systems are sometimes employed to maintain moisture levels, and agrochemicals are applied to keep away pests and disease. Fire prevention would not be your primary concern, as it would in a natural forest.

Fires are a primary concern of forest fire inspectors and prevention specialists. In this job, you would enforce laws relating to fire prevention and inspect forests for potential **fire hazards**. In a state or national park, you might drive around and make sure that campers and other recreational users of the park are obeying the rules. In some places, campfires will be forbidden; in others, there will be rules for putting out fires safely. It will be your job to see that campers adhere to these rules. You would also watch for signs

▲ Forest firefighters will sometimes deliberately set fires in order to stop a blaze from progressing.

of smoke while out on patrol. Quick intervention is necessary to prevent a forest fire from getting out of control.

When a blaze does occur, local firefighters are brought in to contain it. If they are unsuccessful, firefighters from other regions are flown in. A very large forest fire can involve firefighters from around the country. Firefighters who battle wildfires employ different methods from those used against fires in buildings. Helicopters and airplanes are used to drop water and flame retardant chemicals on the fire from above. Controlled fires are deliberately set in the fire's path to create a fire break to stop the blaze from progressing. Firefighters travel ahead of the blaze, anticipating which way it will move next and evacuating residents in its path.

Who's Hiring?

- USDA Forest Service

- Municipal fire departments

- State governments

- Privately owned forests

Where Are the Jobs?

Your job environment will vary by climate and by type of employer. If you are a forestry aide for a national or state forest, you will spend most of your time outside engaged in fire prevention activities and maintenance work. You may drive a vehicle on patrol, or find yourself stationed at a particular lookout post. Your job may involve interaction with visitors, and it may involve keeping records of what you have seen and done during your workday.

TALKING TRENDS

Although overall employment prospects in the forest sector are expected to increase more slowly than average, forestry jobs that relate to the prevention of forest fires may be an exception, particularly in areas with drier climates, and any areas where residential building is encroaching on habitat that is prone to destructive fires.

Firefighters can expect to see faster than average job growth, but this trend is somewhat offset by the keen competition for jobs. Firefighting is a popular occupational choice for people with only a high school degree due to its challenge, importance, respect, high pay, and guaranteed pension.

If you are a firefighter for the USDA Forest Service, you will work outside fighting wild-fires that are burning trees or brush. Your work may take you into different climates and terrains; the area may be flat, but it most likely will be steep. You will be working along the edges of inhabited areas, creating fire lines and breaks to prevent the spread of fires into areas with dwellings and other manmade things.

You might also work as a **municipal** firefighter. In this case, your work environment will consist of your fire station, until you are called to put out a fire or perform some type of rescue operation. Municipal firefighters are called to assist with wildfires, but their primary task is putting out fires in buildings. If you live in an urban area, your opportunities for working on

▲ Clearing brush from roads is one way to prevent a fire from spreading.

wildfires may be few and far between. If you live in a municipality that is adjacent to wild-fire-prone areas, fighting wildfires may constitute a major part of your duties.

Firefighters work long shifts and are often required to work on holidays. Some depart-ments arrange shifts in a 24 hours on–48 hours off schedule. Others have 10- to 14-hour days or work night shifts for three to four days or nights in a row, followed by three to four days off, and then the cycle repeats.

Regardless of the schedule or workplace, one thing that is common to all firefighting jobs is the protective gear that you have to wear. It is hot and incredibly heavy, something that you will have to get used to.

A Typical Day

Here are the highlights for a typical day for a USDA Forest Service firefighter.

Report to the fire station and wait. When your shift starts, you need to be at the fire station. If you are not called to any fires, you may stay there, cleaning, inspecting equipment, engaging in practice drills, playing cards, cooking, napping, or watching television, for your entire shift.

Inspect your gear and get it ready. If you are called to a fire, you need to be able to get to it with all possible speed. Your equipment must be in working order and set out, ready to go in an instant. Your boots are literally set beside the engine, waiting for you to step into them as you climb on board.

Receive orders on how to tackle the fire. If your unit is called to a fire during your shift, you will need to listen to the orders of your superiors. Once you have experience fighting fires for many years, you will be the one giving the orders. You may be asked to attack the fires with water, dig a fire line, burn a fire break, evacuate residents, provide backup support to other units, or any number of other related tasks.

Start Preparing Now

- Work out. This is a job that requires you to be in top physical condition, with exceptional strength, stamina, coordination, and agility. Running and lifting weights are both good activities to improve your fitness.

- Take courses in fire science or emergency medicine at your local community college. Any related coursework that you have completed will help your application stand out from the crowd.

NOTES FROM THE FIELD

Forest firefighter, San Diego, California

Q: *How did you get your job?*

A: I took fire science and EMT (emergency medical technician) classes at the junior college, went to fire stations to learn more about the job, and put myself in the best physical shape I could. I applied for two cities and literally had to stand in line with approximately 7,500 others for over 24 hours for one of them. After the application was accepted, we took a written exam on general common sense, learning abilities, mechanical aptitude, math, spelling, etc. Those who scored in the top group were allowed to take the physical abilities exam. This consisted of pulling hose, dry and charged, carrying and raising ladders, carrying hose, running stairs, pulling hose from the fourth story, and correctly lifting heavy objects and running with them. It was a timed event of doing all sections consecutively to test strength, abilities, and endurance.

Those who passed this exam were then interviewed. I took classes on how to take an interview, and also did mock practice interviews with other firefighters. I tried to get criticism from several different people, from those who were supportive of me and also from those who were against women in the fire service. This way I could be more prepared for the actual interview regardless of who was giving it. After approximately two years of classes, exams, and interviews, I was selected for an academy of 12 people. The academy was stressful and rigorous, and looking back now, it was great fun. But at the time, I think most were extremely stressed. Three people failed but made it almost to the very end before they did. Several were injured during the academy, one severely. Once on the job, we were put on a training crew for several months, then allowed out into the ranks as a **probationary** firefighter. Written critiques after every shift were put in our files. After three annual exams, we would receive a promotion to firefighter 2 and be allowed to work on a promotion to the next level or for a specialty, like Hazardous Materials, EOD, etc.

Q: *What do you like best about your job?*

A: I loved the teamwork, the **camaraderie**, the continuous training to better ourselves. I loved being hands-on with helping people, and the excitement of fighting fires. It is a very important job, and one has to want to do their very best at all times to do well.

Q: *What's the most challenging part of your job?*

A: For me as a woman in the fire service, the most challenging part personally was acceptance by those I was working with. Each day you can work with a new crew member who is not open and accepting of anyone who is not "one of them." So these days usually started out a little stressful. But after a few calls, all would be just fine.

Q: *What are the keys to success for being a firefighter?*

A: The most important part of the job is continually learning a newer and better and safer way to handle each type of situation. Everything from helping people with life-threatening contagious diseases, to a faster safer rescue technique for extricating someone from a very dangerous situation, to learning how to recognize the signs of a hazardous material, to bombs.

• Study for the exam. The higher your score, the better your chances of getting an appointment. Use the Web sites at the end of the chapter to get information on how to prepare for the exam.

Training and How to Get It

In order to become a firefighter, you need to undergo a long application and training process. The first step is a written exam. This is followed by rigorous tests of physical strength, stamina, coordination, and agility that simulate situations you would encounter on the job, such as carrying a fire hose up many flights of stairs or evacuating an overweight person from a burning building. You will also have to undergo a medical examination, and drug screening. Random drug screening will continue throughout your employment.

See what it's like to be a wildland firefighter.

The applicants with the highest scores have the best chance of being accepted into the department's training program. You can bolster your chances by taking community college courses in fire science, emergency medicine, or hazardous materials handling.

If you are successful in getting an appointment, the next step will be attending your department's training academy. Like the exam, this will be an arduous weeding out process. You will spend time both in the classroom and on practical training learning both fire prevention and firefighting techniques, how to handle hazardous materials, and local building codes. Firefighter trainees must also study emergency procedures, first aid, and CPR (cardiopulmonary resuscitation). All firefighters must have at least EMT-Basic certification. Some larger departments are now requiring certification. If you can get this certification on your own before you apply, you will have an advantage over other applicants. For the more practical side of your training, you will learn to use standard firefighting equipment, such as ladders, hoses, fire extinguishers, chainsaws, axes, and rescue equipment.

After your basic training, you will be assigned to a fire company for a probationary period. Your training will continue here under a four-year apprenticeship program. Your on-the-job training will be supplemented with formal instruction in firefighting techniques, equipment usage, hazardous chemicals and building materials, emergency medicine, and fire prevention and safety.

As you get more experience, you will be able to take advantage of local advanced training programs and sessions administered by the U.S. National Fire Academy. These sessions will help you develop leadership skills, such as management, disaster preparedness, and fire safety education. Also your department may provide tuition reimbursement for two- or four-year degrees in fire science or fire engineering. Advanced training may lead to higher pay and the opportunity to move up the ranks.

Promotion is usually dependent upon performance on written examinations and simulations of firefighting scenarios at assessment centers. The best candidates for promotion are carefully screened, and a bachelor's degree in fire science or a related field, or an associate's degree from the National Fire Academy, may be necessary for positions above battalion chief.

Formal training is not the only prerequisite to being a firefighter. There are also personal qualities that are essential for this demanding job. You and other members of your crew will depend upon one another in dangerous situations. Above all, you must exercise good judgment and alertness, self-discipline, endurance, and courage. You must be strong, coordinated, agile, and have mechanical aptitude. In addition, it is essential that higher-ranking officers exhibit leadership qualities. They engage in public speaking, management, budgeting, and public relations, so an aptitude for and willingness to learn these skills is compulsory.

▲ A team of forest firefighters put out hotspots.

Learn the Lingo

Here are a few terms of the trade:

- **Nomex** A special flame-retardant material used to make the clothing worn by firefighters.

- **Pulaski** A standard wildfire fighting tool that looks like a combination of an axe and a hoe. A Pulaski is used for digging fire lines and cutting through tree roots.

- **Ladder fire** When fire-burning foliage on the forest floor jumps into the tree branches, this is called a ladder fire.

Finding a Job

The majority of forestry-related jobs are in the western part of the country, where most national and private forests are located. The main employer in this field is the USDA Forest Service. There are also jobs to be found working in state and private forests. Check your state government's Web site and search the Internet for information on large forests where you live. For firefighting opportunities it is best to check with towns and cities in your area. Experience from volunteer work can be invaluable in landing your first paying position.

Tips for Success

- Keep your skills up to date. The way that we prepare for and attempt to prevent disasters such as fires, hazardous materials spills, infestations, and other emergencies is continually changing. Advances in technology, psychology, criminology, and biology may affect the options available to you and the decisions that you make. It is essential that you regularly attend training sessions to update your skills.

- Be courteous and thoughtful toward your colleagues—information and teamwork are very important to forestry work.

LEARN MORE ONLINE

INTERNATIONAL ASSOCIATION OF FIREFIGHTERS
Organization that represents firefighters in the United States and Canada. http://client.prod.iaff.org/

U.S. FIRE ADMINISTRATION
Training and education information for firefighters. http://www.usfa.fema.gov

USDA FOREST SERVICE
Federal government site that contains detailed maps and information about national forests by state and name, as well as job listings. http://www.fs.fed.us

Reality Check

Firefighting is an intense, physically demanding, and dangerous occupation. According to the National Interagency Fire Commission, 155 wildland firefighters were killed between 2007 and 2016.

Related Jobs to Consider

Emergency medical technician (EMT). EMTs are trained in emergency medicine. They respond to 911 calls and accompany firefighters to fires. This job requires professional certification and a strong stomach. You must also be physically strong, as you will have to lift people and heavy equipment.

Forest conservation worker. Forest conservation workers perform a variety of duties related to maintaining forest health or maintaining roads, campsites, and other facilities for human use. This occupation is virtually identical to that of forestry aide.

How to Move Up

- The next step up from being a forestry aide would be to become a professional forester. Many colleges, as well as vocational and technical schools, offer training programs in forestry, conservation, and wildlife management.

- The profession of firefighting has a clear hierarchical line of promotion going from engineer to lieutenant, then captain, battalion chief, assistant chief, deputy chief, and, at the top, chief. While experience and examination results used to be the main criteria for promotion, fire departments are increasingly looking for a bachelor's degree in fire science or a related field for promotion above the battalion chief level.

TEXT-DEPENDENT QUESTIONS

1. *What kind of training is required in this field?*

2. *What is a Pulaski?*

3. *How might one move up in this field?*

4. *What are some related jobs you might consider?*

RESEARCH PROJECTS

1. *Find out what it's really like to be a forest firefighter by reading one of these books:* Smokejumper *by Jason A. Ramos;* Fire on the Mountain *by John Maclean;* The Fire Line *by Fernanda Santos. Or listen to this interview with a forest firefighter about what his job entails: http://www.npr.org/templates/story/story.php?storyId=112440766*

2. *Stay on top of what's going on in wildland fires by following the news section at Wildland Fires (www.wildlandfires.com). Look up your home state on their state links page (http://www.wildlandfire.com/links) and find out more about forest-fire prevention efforts in your area.*

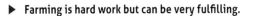

▶ Farming is hard work but can be very fulfilling.

preparation 7
    animal control officer 35, 38–39
    butcher 53
    conservation 78
    farmworker 16
    fish cleaner 53
    forest firefighter 102, 104
    forestry 78
    greenhouse assistant 90
    groundskeeper 66
    landscaper 66
    livestock farmer 28
    logging-crew member 78
    meat-processer 53
    nursery assistant 90
    pest control technician 35, 38–39
    range aide 102, 104
    tree trimmer 66

promotion
    animal control officer 44
    butcher 56–57
    conservation 83
    farmworker 18
    fish cleaner 56–57
    forest firefighter 103, 105, 108
    forestry 83
    greenhouse assistant 95
    groundskeeper 70
    landscaper 70
    livestock farmer 31
    logging-crew member 82–83
    meat-processer 56–57
    nursery assistant 95
    pest control technician 44
    range aide 108
    tree trimmer 70

salary
    animal control officer 35
    butcher 48
    conservation 74
    farmworker 10, 17–18
    fish cleaner 48
    forest firefighter 98
    forestry 74
    greenhouse assistant 86
    groundskeeper 60
    livestock farmer
    logging-crew member 74
    meat-processer 48
    nursery assistant 86
    pest control technician 35

range aide 98
    tree trimmer 60

training 6–7
    animal control officer 39, 44
    butcher 54
    farmworker 16–17
    fish cleaner 54
    forest firefighter 103–105, 107
    greenhouse assistant 89, 90–91, 93–94
    groundskeeper 66–67
    landscaper 66–67, 69
    livestock farmer 28–29, 31
    logging-crew member 79, 82–83
    meat-processer 54
    nursery assistant 89, 90–91, 93–94
    pest control technician 39
    range aide 108

trends
    animal control officer 37
    butcher 51
    farmworker 13
    fish cleaner 51
    forest firefighter 100
    forestry 77, 100
    greenhouse assistant 88
    groundskeeper 62
    livestock farmer 26
    logging-crew member 77
    meat-processer 51
    nursery assistant 88
    pest control technician 37
    range aide 100

work environment 6
    animal control officer 36–37
    butcher 48–49, 56
    conservation 77
    farmworker 17–18
    fish cleaner 48
    forest firefighter 101
    forestry 77
    greenhouse assistant 88–89
    groundskeeper 62–63
    landscaper 63, 69
    livestock farmer 22–24
    logging-crew member 77
    meat-processer 48–49
    nursery assistant 88–89
    pest control technician 37
    range aide 100
    tree trimmer 63

A butcher must know how to judge the quality of meats and when they are prime for eating.

Cover

(Central image) ViktorCap/iStock; (top to bottom) 123ducu/iStock, Ismael Mijan/Shutterstock, Halfpoint/iStock, Alpa Prod/Shutterstock, LaraBelova/iStock

Interior

4 (left to right), Jenoche/Shutterstock; Ismael Mijan/Shutterstock; Iakov Filimonov/Shutterstock; Alpa Prod/Shutterstock; Andrey Popov/Shutterstock; 7, Kosamtu/iStock; 8, sasimoto/iStock; 11, dmaroscar/iStock; 12, Josef Mohyla/iStock; 16, oticki/iStock; 20, Iakov Filimonov/Shutterstock; 23, tawatchaiprakobkit/iStock; 24, U.S. Department of Agriculture/Bob Nichols; 25, Chalabala/iStock; 32, hedgehog94/iStock; 35, HighLaZ/iStock; 38, John-Reynolds/iStock; 41, Lisa Eastman/Shutterstock; 42, leezsnow/iStock; 45, sgoodwin4813/iStock; 46, Iakov Filimonov/Shutterstock; 49, piola666/iStock; 50, IP Galanternik D.U./iStock; 52, Wavebreakmedia/iStock; 55, Lokibaho/iStock; 58, juefraphoto/iStock; 61, schulzie/iStock; 63, kbwills/iStock; 64, EJ-J/iStock; 68, jjjroy/iStock; 71, JFsPic/iStock; 72, fesoj/iStock; 75, Josef Mohyla/iStock; 78, U.S. Department of Agriculture; 81, abadonian/iStock; 84, pixdeluxe/iStock; 87, Darwel/iStock; 89, Vladimir Vladimirov/iStock; 92, U.S. Department of Agriculture/Lance Cheung; 96, U.S. Department of Agriculture; 99, U.S. Department of Agriculture; 101, U.S. Department of Agriculture; 106, U.S. Department of Agriculture; 109, ProductionPerig/Dreamstime; 111, Tyler Olson/Dreamstime